The Lifelong Learning Blueprint:
Unlocking Personal and Professional Growth

OrangeBooks Publication

1st Floor, Rajhans Arcade, Mall Road, Kohka, Bhilai, Chhattisgarh 490020

Website: **www.orangebooks.in**

© **Copyright, 2024, Author**

All rights reserved. No part of this book may be reproduced, stored in a retrieval system, or transmitted, in any form by any means, electronic, mechanical, magnetic, optical, chemical, manual, photocopying, recording or otherwise, without the prior written consent of its writer.

First Edition, 2024

ISBN: 978-93-6554-537-1

THE LIFELONG LEARNING BLUEPRINT

UNLOCKING PERSONAL AND PROFESSIONAL GROWTH

SAURABH K & DEEP SIKHA

OrangeBooks Publication
www.orangebooks.in

Dedication

To my family, whose unwavering support and love have been the bedrock of my journey.

To my parents, who taught me the value of learning and perseverance, and whose wisdom continues to guide me every day.

To my wife (Deepu), whose boundless belief in my aspirations has been my greatest strength.

To my sister and brother-in-law (Shabnam & Anjan), for standing by me with encouragement and shared dreams.

And to my love Duggu, whose innocent smiles remind me daily of the joy and beauty in life.

And finally, to everyone who believes in the power of continuous growth and the pursuit of knowledge your faith in me has made this book possible. Thank you for being my inspiration.

Acknowledgments

I would like to express my deepest gratitude to the people who have been my pillars of strength and inspiration throughout this journey.

To my parents, thank you for instilling in me the values of hard work, perseverance, and the importance of education. Your unwavering support and encouragement have always guided me.

To my loving wife (Deep Sikha), your belief in me has been my greatest motivation. Thank you for your endless patience, understanding, and for always standing by my side as I pursue my dreams.

To my family, your love and encouragement have been my anchor. I am grateful for your constant support and for reminding me of the importance of lifelong learning in both personal and professional life.

This book is a reflection of the lessons you've all taught me, and I am forever grateful.

In Loving Honor To My Parents

Amrendra Kumar

For being the guiding light in my life, teaching me the values of hard work, integrity, and the relentless pursuit of knowledge. Your wisdom has shaped the person I am today.

Sudha Kumari

For your endless love, patience, and the life lessons you've imparted. Your nurturing spirit and strength have been my greatest source of comfort and inspiration.

This book is a testament to the values you both instilled in me, and I am forever grateful for your unwavering support.

Inspiring Words on Lifelong Learning

Timeless Quotes from Visionary Leaders

In the journey of lifelong learning, wisdom from those who have shaped history can serve as both guide and inspiration. These selected quotes from renowned leaders highlight the transformative power of continuous growth and the enduring value of education, urging us all to embrace learning at every stage of life.

1. *"Live as if you were to die tomorrow. Learn as if you were to live forever."*

   – Mahatma Gandhi

2. *"Anyone who stops learning is old, whether at twenty or eighty. Anyone who keeps learning stays young."*

   – Henry Ford

3. *"The illiterate of the 21st century will not be those who cannot read and write, but those who cannot learn, unlearn, and relearn."*

   – Alvin Toffler

4. *"Education is the most powerful weapon which you can use to change the world."*

   – Nelson Mandela

5. *"In a time of drastic change, it is the learners who inherit the future. The learned usually find themselves equipped to live in a world that no longer exists."*
   – Eric Hoffer

6. *"Learning never exhausts the mind."*
   – Leonardo da Vinci

7. *"The only thing worse than training your employees and having them leave is not training them and having them stay."*
   – Henry Ford

8. *"Change is the end result of all true learning."*
   – Leo Buscaglia

9. *"A love of reading, the habit of getting a feel of knowledge, will last you all your life."*
   – Thomas Jefferson

10. *"An investment in knowledge pays the best interest."*
    – Benjamin Franklin

Purpose and Audience Breakdown

1. Professionals and Freshers Seeking Career Advancement

- **Purpose:** Offer strategies for continuous skill development and career growth.
- **Needs:** Practical advice on identifying and acquiring new skills, networking, and staying relevant in their field.

Content Focus:

- How to assess and identify skills needed for career advancement.
- Strategies for leveraging online courses, certifications, and workshops.
- Tips for networking and professional development.

2. Retirees Looking for New Passions

- **Purpose:** Provide guidance on finding and pursuing new interests and passions after retirement.
- **Needs:** Ideas for engaging in new learning opportunities, hobbies, or even second careers.

Content Focus:

- ➤ Exploring new hobbies, volunteering, and educational pursuits.
- ➤ Success stories of retirees who have reinvented themselves.
- ➤ Practical steps for starting new learning adventures.

3. Lifelong Learners in General

- ➤ **Purpose:** Encourage and guide individuals in maintaining a continuous learning mindset throughout life.
- ➤ **Needs:** Inspiration and practical methods for integrating learning into daily routines.

Content Focus:

- ➤ Strategies for maintaining curiosity and motivation.
- ➤ Tips for incorporating learning into busy schedules.
- ➤ Examples of diverse learning methods and resources.

Content

Introduction 1

➢ Purpose of the Book 1
  How This Book Will Help You Achieve Personal Growth
  and Career Advancement 2

➢ Why Lifelong Learning Matters 3
  Benefits of Continuous Learning for Various Life Stages . 4
  Overview of Key Topics Covered in the Book 5

1. Understanding Lifelong Learning 8

➢ Defining Lifelong Learning 8
  Lifelong Learning: A Comprehensive Definition 8
  Different Forms of Lifelong Learning 11

➢ The Growth Mindset 15
  Introduction to the Concept of a Growth Mindset 15
  How Adopting a Growth Mindset Can Enhance Learning
  and Personal Development 19

2. Strategies for Career Advancement 23

➢ For Professionals 23
  Identifying and Acquiring New Skills Relevant to
  Career Growth 23
  For Professionals: Utilizing Professional Development
  Resources 27

➢ For Freshers 33
  How to Assess and Plan for Career-Related Learning ... 33

Tips for Building a Strong Foundation Through Early Learning Experiences...39

3. Exploring Learning Methods 46

➢ **Formal Education** 46
Advantages of Traditional Degrees and Certifications..46
How to Choose the Right Educational Path 52

➢ **Online Learning and Courses** 57
Overview of Popular Online Learning Platforms 57
Tips for Selecting High-Quality Online Courses and Programs..63

➢ **Self-Directed Learning** 69
Techniques for Self-Study and Independent Learning...69
Using Books, Podcasts, and Other Resources Effectively..75

➢ **Experiential Learning** 82
Learning Through Practical Experience and Real-World Applications...82
Examples of How Hands-On Experiences Can Enhance Learning...88

4. Integrating Learning into Daily Life......................93

➢ **Creating a Learning Routine** 93
Practical Tips for Incorporating Learning into a Busy Schedule..93
Setting Realistic Learning Goals and Milestones............98

➢ **Finding Learning Opportunities in Everyday Life** 104
Using Daily Experiences as Learning Opportunities 104
Incorporating Learning into Hobbies, Travel, and Social Interactions..110

5. Overcoming Learning Challenges 116

- **Common Obstacles** 116
  Identifying and Addressing Barriers to Lifelong Learning 116

- **Strategies for Staying Motivated** 123
  Techniques for Maintaining Enthusiasm and Commitment to Learning 123

- **Dealing with Setbacks:** 129
  How to Overcome Setbacks and Stay on Track with Learning Goals 129

6. Inspiring Stories of Transformation 137

- **Success Stories** 137
  Profiles of Individuals Who Have Achieved Significant Personal Growth Through Lifelong Learning 137

- **Lessons Learned** 145
  Key Takeaways and Common Themes from the Stories 145
  How Readers Can Apply These Lessons to Their Own Lives 148

7. Leveraging Technology for Learning 154

- **Digital Tools and Resources** 154
  Overview of Useful Apps, Platforms, and Tools for Learning 154
  How to Effectively Use Technology to Enhance the Learning Experience 158

- **Staying Updated with Technology Trends** 163
  Keeping Up with Emerging Technologies and Their Impact on Learning 163

8. Crafting Your Personal Learning Plan 169

- **Developing a Learning Strategy** 169
  - *Steps for Creating a Personalized Learning Plan.........169*
  - *Setting Short-Term and Long-Term Learning Goals....174*

- **Tracking Progress** 179
  - *Tools and Techniques for Monitoring Learning Progress and Adjusting Goals 179*

- **Building a Support System** 185
  - *Finding Mentors, Peers, and Communities to Support Your Learning Journey..185*

Conclusion 191

Embracing Lifelong Learning 191
- *Summary of Key Takeaways 191*
- *Encouragement for Ongoing Learning.........................195*

- **Call to Action** 198
  - *Motivational Message 200*

Appendices 201
- *Resources and Tools...201*

- **Templates and Worksheets** 205
- **Glossary of Terms** 209

A Note of Thanks 215

Introduction

Purpose of the Book

Lifelong learning is more than just a buzzword; it's a philosophy that empowers individuals to continuously evolve, both personally and professionally. In a world that's rapidly changing, the ability to adapt and grow through learning has become crucial for success. This book is designed to introduce you to the concept of lifelong learning, showing how it can unlock doors to new opportunities, enhance your skills, and bring fulfilment at every stage of life.

Lifelong learning isn't limited to formal education or structured environments. It's about staying curious, embracing new experiences, and continually seeking knowledge, whether you're advancing in your career, pursuing a passion, or simply looking to expand your horizons. Through this book, you'll discover practical strategies and inspirational stories that will help you integrate learning into your daily life, overcome obstacles, and ultimately achieve the personal and professional growth you desire.

This book aims to inspire you to take control of your learning journey, offering guidance on how to develop a growth mindset, set meaningful goals, and explore various learning methods. Whether you're a professional looking to climb the career ladder, a recent graduate seeking direction, or someone who believes in the power of education at any age, this book is your companion on the path to lifelong learning.

How This Book Will Help You Achieve Personal Growth and Career Advancement

In today's fast-paced world, the ability to learn and adapt is more important than ever. Whether you're a seasoned professional or just starting out, the skills and knowledge you acquire through lifelong learning will set you apart and propel you toward your goals. This book is designed to provide you with the tools and insights needed to harness the power of lifelong learning in a practical, actionable way.

Here's how this book will support your journey:

1. **Personal Growth:** You'll learn how to cultivate a growth mindset, enabling you to embrace challenges, overcome obstacles, and continuously expand your capabilities. The book will offer strategies for integrating learning into your daily life, helping you build confidence, resilience, and a sense of fulfilment.

2. **Career Advancement:** The book will guide you in identifying and acquiring the skills most relevant to your career goals. Whether it's mastering new technologies, enhancing soft skills, or pursuing formal education and certifications, you'll find practical advice on how to stay competitive in your field. By continuously learning, you'll be better

equipped to seize new opportunities, adapt to changes, and advance in your career.

3. **Real-Life Examples and Inspirational Stories:** Throughout the book, you'll encounter stories of individuals who have transformed their lives through lifelong learning. These examples will not only inspire you but also provide concrete lessons that you can apply to your own life.

4. **Customized Learning Strategies:** You'll be introduced to various learning methods—formal education, online courses, self-directed study, and experiential learning—and guided on how to choose the path that best suits your needs. The book will also help you develop a personalized learning plan, set realistic goals, and track your progress.

By the end of this book, you'll have a comprehensive understanding of lifelong learning and how to leverage it to achieve your personal and professional aspirations. Whether your aim is to climb the corporate ladder, find new passions in retirement, or simply keep your mind sharp and engaged, this book will be your roadmap to a life of continuous growth and success.

Why Lifelong Learning Matters

In an ever-changing world, the ability to learn continuously is not just an asset—it's a necessity. Lifelong learning empowers you to adapt to new challenges, seize opportunities, and lead a more fulfilling life, regardless of your age or stage in life.

Let's explore why lifelong learning is so crucial and how it benefits you at various points in your journey.

Benefits of Continuous Learning for Various Life Stages

1. For Professionals: As industries evolve and technology advances, staying relevant requires more than just maintaining your current skills. Lifelong learning helps you stay ahead of the curve, enabling you to acquire new competencies, advance in your career, and adapt to emerging trends. Whether it's through formal education, professional development courses, or self-directed learning, continuous education ensures that you remain competitive in your field.

2. **For Freshers:** Starting out in your career can be overwhelming, but a commitment to lifelong learning gives you a distinct advantage. By embracing new learning opportunities, you can build a strong foundation of skills and knowledge that will propel you forward. Early investment in learning can also help you navigate career choices, discover your passions, and set the stage for long-term success.

3. **For Retirees and Lifelong Learners:** Retirement doesn't mean the end of learning; in fact, it can be the beginning of a new chapter. Lifelong learning keeps your mind sharp, introduces you to new hobbies or interests, and even opens doors to second careers or volunteer opportunities. It's a powerful way to stay engaged, connected, and fulfilled as you explore new passions and continue to grow.

4. **For Everyone:** Beyond career and professional benefits, lifelong learning enriches your personal life. It fosters curiosity, creativity, and a sense of purpose. Whether you're learning a new language, mastering a musical instrument, or exploring new philosophies, continuous learning helps you grow as an individual, expand your worldview, and connect with others.

Overview of Key Topics Covered in the Book

This book is designed to be your comprehensive guide to lifelong learning, offering practical advice, strategies, and inspiration tailored to your unique needs and goals. Here's an overview of what you can expect:

1. **Understanding Lifelong Learning:** We'll start by defining what lifelong learning is and why it's essential in today's world. You'll learn about different forms of learning, from formal education to self-directed study, and how each can play a role in your growth.

2. **Cultivating a Growth Mindset:** Adopting a growth mindset is key to embracing challenges and persisting in the face of setbacks. This section will introduce you to the concept and provide strategies for developing a mindset that fuels continuous learning.

3. **Exploring Learning Methods:** Whether you prefer traditional education, online courses, or experiential learning, we'll explore various methods to help you find the best fit for your learning style and goals. You'll gain insights into how to choose high-quality

programs and effectively use resources like books, podcasts, and hands-on experiences.

4. **Integrating Learning into Daily Life:** Lifelong learning doesn't have to be a chore; it can be seamlessly integrated into your everyday life. This part of the book will offer practical tips for creating a learning routine, setting realistic goals, and finding learning opportunities in your daily experiences.

5. **Overcoming Learning Challenges:** Every learning journey has obstacles. Whether it's a lack of time, motivation, or resources, this section will equip you with strategies to overcome common barriers and stay motivated on your path.

6. **Inspiring Stories of Transformation:** To inspire and motivate you, we'll share success stories of individuals from various backgrounds who have achieved significant personal growth through lifelong learning. These stories will offer valuable lessons and demonstrate the transformative power of continuous learning.

7. **Leveraging Technology for Learning:** In today's digital age, technology offers countless tools and resources to enhance your learning experience. We'll explore the best apps, platforms, and digital tools to support your lifelong learning journey.

8. **Crafting Your Personal Learning Plan:** Finally, the book will guide you in creating a personalized learning plan that aligns with your goals and aspirations. You'll learn how to set short-term and

long-term goals, track your progress, and build a support system to sustain your learning journey.

By the end of this book, you'll have a clear understanding of why lifelong learning matters and how you can make it an integral part of your life. You'll be equipped with the knowledge, tools, and inspiration to embark on a journey of continuous growth, ensuring that you live a life filled with purpose, fulfilment, and success.

Chapter 1
Understanding Lifelong Learning

Defining Lifelong Learning

Lifelong Learning: A Comprehensive Definition

Lifelong learning refers to the ongoing, voluntary, and self-motivated pursuit of knowledge for personal or professional development. Unlike formal education, which typically concludes with graduation, lifelong learning is a continuous process that extends throughout an individual's life. It encompasses a wide range of activities, from formal courses and certifications to self-directed study and experiential learning.

Why Lifelong Learning Matters

In today's rapidly changing world, lifelong learning is not just beneficial but essential. Here's why it's important:

1. **Adapting to Change:**
   - ➤ **Example:** Sarah, a mid-career professional in marketing, faced a significant shift as digital marketing technologies evolved. By engaging in online courses and webinars about social media strategies and data analytics, she not only stayed relevant but advanced her career. Lifelong

learning helped Sarah adapt to industry changes and position herself as a thought leader.

2. **Enhancing Career Opportunities:**
   - ➢ **Example:** Raj, a recent college graduate, started in a junior software developer role. He realized that gaining additional skills in machine learning and data science could open doors to more advanced roles. By dedicating time to online courses and projects, Raj was able to transition to a senior data scientist position within a few years.

3. **Personal Fulfillment and Growth:**
   - ➢ **Example:** Maria, a retired school teacher, always had a passion for painting but never had time to explore it fully during her career. After retirement, she took art classes and found immense personal satisfaction and a new sense of purpose. Lifelong learning allowed Maria to pursue her passion and experience personal growth well into her retirement.

4. **Building Resilience:**
   - ➢ **Example:** John, who was laid off from his job, faced uncertainty and stress. Instead of viewing this as a setback, he used the opportunity to learn new skills in project management and entrepreneurship. This proactive approach not only helped him secure a new position but also equipped him with skills to navigate future uncertainties with confidence.

5. **Fostering Curiosity and Innovation:**
    - ➤ **Example:** Lisa, a tech entrepreneur, continually seeks out new knowledge in emerging technologies and business strategies. Her commitment to learning has led to innovative ideas and successful ventures. Lifelong learning fuels Lisa's curiosity and drives her to explore new possibilities.

Key Aspects of Lifelong Learning

1. **Continuous Learning:** Lifelong learning is an ongoing process that doesn't end with formal education. It involves regularly seeking new knowledge and skills to keep up with changes and seize opportunities.

2. **Self-Motivation:** Unlike structured academic settings, lifelong learning requires self-motivation. Individuals must take initiative and drive their own learning journeys.

3. **Diverse Learning Methods:** Lifelong learning is not confined to traditional classroom settings. It includes online courses, workshops, self-study, reading, and learning from experiences and interactions.

4. **Personal and Professional Development:** Lifelong learning encompasses both personal interests and professional skills. It's about enhancing one's knowledge base, skill set, and overall development.

5. **Adaptability:** As the world changes, so do the skills and knowledge required. Lifelong learning helps

individuals remain adaptable and competitive in their fields.

Conclusion

Lifelong learning is more than just a buzzword; it's a critical component of personal and professional success in today's dynamic world. By understanding and embracing lifelong learning, individuals can stay relevant, achieve their goals, and find fulfillment throughout their lives. Whether you're a young professional seeking career advancement, a retiree exploring new passions, or a lifelong learner eager to expand your horizons, lifelong learning offers valuable opportunities for growth and transformation.

By adopting a mindset of continuous learning, you empower yourself to face challenges with confidence, embrace new opportunities, and achieve a richer, more fulfilling life.

Different Forms of Lifelong Learning

Lifelong learning encompasses a variety of approaches, each offering unique benefits and catering to different needs and preferences. Understanding these forms can help you choose the best method to suit your personal and professional goals.

1. Formal Learning

What It Is: Formal learning refers to structured educational experiences provided by accredited institutions, such as schools, colleges, universities, and professional training centres. It follows a set curriculum and is often credentialed, leading to degrees, diplomas, or certifications.

Why It Matters:

> **Structured Curriculum:** Provides a well-organized and comprehensive learning experience.

> **Accreditation and Credentials:** Offers recognized qualifications that can enhance career prospects and professional credibility.

> **Expert Instruction:** Delivered by trained educators or industry professionals with expertise in the subject matter.

Example: Emily, an engineer with a few years of experience, decided to pursue a Master's degree in Data Science. The formal education provided her with a deep understanding of data analytics and machine learning, along with a recognized degree that opened new career opportunities in advanced data roles.

2. Informal Learning

What It Is: Informal learning occurs outside of traditional educational settings and does not follow a structured curriculum. It includes learning through everyday experiences, social interactions, and media consumption. Examples include reading books, watching educational videos, attending seminars, or engaging in discussions with peers.

Why It Matters:

- **Flexibility:** Allows you to learn at your own pace and according to your interests.
- **Relevance:** Often focuses on practical, real-world knowledge that can be immediately applied.
- **Accessibility:** Easier to access and often free or low-cost.

Example: Tom, a marketing manager, enjoys listening to industry podcasts during his commute. By following podcasts from leading marketing experts and thought leaders, Tom stays updated on the latest trends and strategies without committing to formal coursework.

3. Self-Directed Learning

What It Is: Self-directed learning is an autonomous approach where individuals take responsibility for their own learning process. It involves setting personal learning goals, choosing resources, and evaluating progress. This form of learning is highly personalized and often driven by individual interests and needs.

Why It Matters:

- **Personalization:** Tailors learning experiences to fit your specific interests and goals.
- **Autonomy:** Empowers you to take control of your learning journey and make decisions based on your preferences.
- **Adaptability:** Allows you to quickly adjust learning methods and focus areas based on changing needs and new information.

Example: Sophie, a graphic designer, wanted to enhance her skills in digital illustration. She set personal learning goals, selected online tutorials, and practiced regularly. Through self-directed learning, Sophie mastered new techniques and expanded her creative toolkit, directly benefiting her work and client projects.

Comparing the Forms

> ➤ **Formal Learning** provides a structured pathway and credentials but can be time-consuming and costly. It is ideal for acquiring comprehensive knowledge and qualifications.

> ➤ **Informal Learning** is flexible and cost-effective, suitable for continuous, day-to-day learning and staying updated on relevant topics.

> ➤ **Self-Directed Learning** offers autonomy and personalization, allowing individuals to tailor their learning experiences but requiring self-motivation and discipline.

Conclusion

Understanding the different forms of lifelong learning helps you choose the methods that best align with your goals and learning style. Whether you opt for formal education, engage in informal learning, or pursue self-directed learning, each form plays a vital role in fostering personal and professional growth. By leveraging these various approaches, you can create a dynamic and fulfilling learning journey that supports continuous development throughout your life.

The Growth Mindset

Introduction to the Concept of a Growth Mindset

The concept of a growth mindset, introduced by psychologist Carol Dweck, revolutionizes how we think about learning and personal development. It contrasts sharply with a fixed mindset and has profound implications for how we approach challenges, setbacks, and opportunities for growth.

What Is a Growth Mindset?

A growth mindset is the belief that abilities and intelligence can be developed through dedication, hard work, and learning. People with a growth mindset embrace challenges, persist through difficulties, and view failures as opportunities to grow rather than as reflections of their limitations.

Core Principles of a Growth Mindset:

1. **Belief in Development:**
   - **Explanation:** Individuals with a growth mindset believe that their talents and intelligence are not fixed traits but can be developed through effort and learning.
   - **Example:** Alex, a software developer, struggled with a new programming language. Instead of believing he was inherently bad at it, he dedicated time to practice and seek help. His perseverance led to mastering the language and applying it successfully in his projects.

2. Embracing Challenges:

- **Explanation:** Those with a growth mindset view challenges as opportunities to improve and learn, rather than obstacles to avoid.

- **Example:** Priya, a marketing executive, was tasked with leading a major campaign outside her comfort zone. Embracing the challenge, she researched extensively and collaborated with colleagues. The campaign was a success, and Priya gained valuable experience and confidence.

3. Persistence in the Face of Setbacks:

- **Explanation:** People with a growth mindset understand that setbacks and failures are a natural part of the learning process and use them as learning experiences.

- **Example:** James, a freelance writer, faced multiple rejections from publishers. Rather than giving up, he revised his manuscript based on feedback and continued submitting. His persistence eventually led to his book being published.

4. Learning from Criticism:

- **Explanation:** Constructive criticism is seen as valuable feedback rather than a personal attack. Individuals with a growth mindset use it to refine their skills and improve their performance.

> **Example:** Emma, an aspiring artist, received critical feedback on her artwork from a mentor. Instead of feeling discouraged, she used the feedback to make improvements and develop her unique style.

5. **Celebrating Others' Successes:**
   > **Explanation:** A growth mindset involves appreciating and learning from the successes of others rather than feeling threatened by them.

   > **Example:** Carlos, a young entrepreneur, admired the achievements of established business leaders. He studied their strategies and sought mentorship, which helped him grow his own startup successfully.

The Impact of a Growth Mindset

1. **Enhanced Learning and Achievement:**
   > **Explanation:** Adopting a growth mindset leads to greater resilience, creativity, and success in various endeavors. Individuals are more likely to take on challenging tasks and persist through difficulties.

   > **Example:** Linda, a university student, struggled with complex subjects. With a growth mindset, she sought additional resources and support, ultimately improving her grades and understanding of the material.

2. **Positive Influence on Personal and Professional Growth:**
   - ➤ **Explanation:** Embracing a growth mindset fosters continuous personal and professional development. It encourages lifelong learning and adaptation to new situations.
   - ➤ **Example:** Mark, a mid-level manager, embraced a growth mindset by continuously seeking new skills and feedback. This approach helped him advance to an executive role and lead successful projects.

3. **Creating a Growth-Oriented Culture:**
   - ➤ **Explanation:** Cultivating a growth mindset within teams and organizations can lead to a more collaborative, innovative, and resilient work environment.
   - ➤ **Example:** A tech company adopted a growth mindset culture, encouraging employees to take risks and learn from failures. This led to increased creativity and a more dynamic workplace.

Conclusion

The growth mindset is a powerful concept that can transform how we approach learning, challenges, and personal development. By believing in the potential for growth and embracing opportunities to learn, we unlock our capacity for continuous improvement and success. Whether in your personal life, career, or broader pursuits, adopting a growth mindset can lead to profound and lasting benefits, fostering resilience, innovation, and fulfilment.

How Adopting a Growth Mindset Can Enhance Learning and Personal Development

The Power of a Growth Mindset

Adopting a growth mindset can fundamentally transform your approach to learning and personal development. By embracing the belief that abilities and intelligence can be developed through effort and dedication, you set yourself on a path to continuous improvement and success. Here's how a growth mindset can significantly enhance both learning and personal development:

1. Fostering Resilience and Perseverance

Explanation: A growth mindset encourages you to view challenges and setbacks as opportunities for growth rather than as insurmountable obstacles. This perspective helps build resilience, allowing you to persevere through difficulties and maintain motivation.

Example: Anna, an aspiring writer, faced multiple rejections from publishers. Instead of giving up, she refined her manuscript and sought feedback. Her resilience paid off when her book was finally accepted and became a bestseller. Anna's growth mindset was crucial in overcoming setbacks and achieving success.

2. Promoting a Love of Learning

Explanation: When you adopt a growth mindset, you become more curious and enthusiastic about learning new things. This positive attitude towards learning fuels a desire to explore new subjects, acquire new skills, and continuously expand your knowledge base.

Example: James, a software engineer, developed an interest in artificial intelligence. Embracing a growth mindset, he took online courses and participated in workshops to learn about AI. His passion for learning led to the development of innovative projects and career advancement.

3. Encouraging Adaptability and Innovation

Explanation: A growth mindset fosters adaptability by encouraging you to embrace new ideas and approaches. This flexibility enhances your ability to innovate and find creative solutions to problems, leading to personal and professional growth.

Example: Lisa, a marketing professional, faced a rapidly changing industry landscape. By adopting a growth mindset, she embraced new marketing technologies and strategies. Her adaptability and innovative approach helped her stay ahead of competitors and achieve career success.

4. Enhancing Problem-Solving Skills

Explanation: With a growth mindset, you approach problems with a solution-oriented mindset. Instead of being deterred by difficulties, you focus on finding ways to overcome them, leading to improved problem-solving skills.

Example: Raj, a project manager, encountered a complex issue during a critical project. By viewing the problem as an opportunity to learn, he collaborated with his team to develop a creative solution. The successful resolution not only salvaged the project but also enhanced Raj's problem-solving abilities.

5. Building Confidence and Self-Efficacy

Explanation: As you experience success through effort and persistence, your confidence and belief in your abilities grow. A growth mindset reinforces the idea that you can achieve your goals through hard work and dedication.

Example: Emily, a recent graduate, was apprehensive about starting her career. By adopting a growth mindset and focusing on continuous learning and skill development, she gained confidence in her abilities. Her newfound self-efficacy helped her excel in her job and advance in her career.

6. Cultivating a Positive Learning Environment

Explanation: A growth mindset not only benefits individuals but also creates a positive and supportive learning environment. Encouraging a growth mindset within teams or educational settings fosters collaboration, constructive feedback, and mutual support.

Example: A company implemented a growth mindset culture, encouraging employees to view challenges as opportunities for growth. This approach fostered a collaborative environment where team members supported each other and shared knowledge, leading to increased innovation and success.

Conclusion

Adopting a growth mindset can profoundly impact your learning and personal development. By fostering resilience, a love of learning, adaptability, problem-solving skills, confidence, and a positive environment, you unlock your potential for continuous growth and success. Embrace the principles of a growth mindset to enhance your journey of lifelong learning and achieve your personal and professional goals.

Chapter 2
Strategies for Career Advancement

For Professionals

Identifying and Acquiring New Skills Relevant to Career Growth

The Importance of Skill Development

In a dynamic job market, continuous skill development is crucial for career advancement. Professionals who proactively identify and acquire new skills can stay ahead of industry trends, increase their value to employers, and open doors to new opportunities. Here's how to effectively identify and acquire new skills to advance your career:

1. Assess Your Current Skills and Career Goals

Explanation: Begin by evaluating your existing skills, strengths, and areas for improvement. Align this assessment with your career goals to determine which skills are necessary for your next career move.

Steps to Take:

> ➤ **Self-Assessment:** Reflect on your current job performance, gather feedback from colleagues and mentors, and identify gaps in your skill set.

> **Career Goals:** Define your career objectives, whether it's moving into a leadership role, transitioning to a new field, or enhancing your technical expertise.

Example: Sarah, a software engineer aiming for a leadership position, assessed her technical skills and realized she needed to improve her project management and team leadership abilities. She set a goal to develop these skills to align with her career aspirations.

2. Research Industry Trends and Emerging Skills

Explanation: Stay informed about industry trends and emerging skills relevant to your field. This research helps you identify which skills are in demand and which will be valuable in the future.

Steps to Take:

> **Industry Reports:** Read industry reports, articles, and whitepapers to understand current and future trends.

> **Job Market Analysis:** Review job postings and professional profiles to see which skills employers are seeking.

Example: Tom, a digital marketer, noticed a growing demand for expertise in data analytics and artificial intelligence. Recognizing the importance of these skills, he decided to focus on acquiring them to stay competitive in the market.

3. Set Clear Learning Objectives and Create a Plan

Explanation: Establish specific, measurable, achievable, relevant, and time-bound (SMART) objectives for acquiring new skills. Develop a plan that outlines how you will achieve these objectives.

Steps to Take:

- ➤ **SMART Goals:** Define clear learning objectives, such as "Complete a certification course in data analytics within six months."
- ➤ **Action Plan:** Create a plan that includes enrolling in courses, attending workshops, and dedicating time for self-study.

Example: Emily set a goal to enhance her public speaking skills by enrolling in a communication skills workshop and practicing regularly. She created a timeline and tracked her progress to stay on track.

4. Choose the Right Learning Resources

Explanation: Select learning resources that best fit your learning style and objectives. Options include online courses, workshops, certifications, books, and mentorship.

Steps to Take:

- ➤ **Online Courses:** Platforms like Coursera, Udemy, and LinkedIn Learning offer a wide range of courses.
- ➤ **Certifications:** Pursue relevant certifications from recognized institutions or professional bodies.

> **Mentorship:** Seek guidance from mentors who can provide valuable insights and support.

Example: Raj, a financial analyst, chose an online course on advanced financial modeling and a mentorship program with a senior analyst to enhance his skills and gain practical experience.

5. Apply New Skills in Real-World Situations

Explanation: To solidify your learning, apply new skills in real-world scenarios. This practical experience helps reinforce your knowledge and demonstrates your capabilities to employers.

Steps to Take:

> **Projects:** Volunteer for projects or assignments at work that allow you to use your new skills.

> **Freelance Work:** Consider freelance or side projects to gain hands-on experience.

Example: Lisa, an HR professional, applied her newly acquired data analysis skills by leading a project to analyze employee engagement metrics. The successful project showcased her capabilities and contributed to her career advancement.

6. Seek Feedback and Reflect on Your Progress

Explanation: Regularly seek feedback from colleagues, mentors, and supervisors to assess your progress and identify areas for improvement. Reflect on your experiences to continuously refine your skills.

Steps to Take:

> **Feedback:** Request constructive feedback on your performance and skill application.

> **Reflection:** Reflect on your learning journey and adjust your plan as needed to achieve your goals.

Example: Mark, a project manager, sought feedback from his team and supervisor on his leadership skills. He used this feedback to make improvements and track his progress toward becoming a more effective leader.

Conclusion

Identifying and acquiring new skills is essential for career advancement. By assessing your current skills, researching industry trends, setting clear objectives, choosing the right resources, applying new skills, and seeking feedback, you can effectively enhance your career prospects. Embrace these strategies to stay relevant, advance in your career, and achieve your professional goals.

For Professionals: Utilizing Professional Development Resources

Leveraging Professional Development Resources

Professional development resources are essential tools for enhancing your skills, expanding your knowledge, and advancing your career. By strategically utilizing courses, certifications, and workshops, you can stay current in your field, acquire new competencies, and position yourself for future opportunities. Here's how to effectively utilize these resources:

1. Online Courses

What They Are: Online courses offer a flexible and accessible way to learn new skills and gain knowledge. They are available on various platforms, such as Coursera, Udemy, LinkedIn Learning, and edX, covering a wide range of topics.

Benefits:

> - **Flexibility:** Learn at your own pace and on your schedule.
> - **Variety:** Access a wide range of subjects and expertise levels.
> - **Cost-Effective:** Many courses are affordable, and some are free.

Steps to Utilize:

> - **Identify Needs:** Determine which skills or knowledge areas you want to improve.
> - **Research Options:** Explore course offerings on reputable platforms.
> - **Enroll and Engage:** Choose courses that match your goals, and actively participate in the learning process.

Example: Maria, a project coordinator, wanted to enhance her skills in Agile project management. She enrolled in an online course on Agile methodologies, which allowed her to complete the coursework at her own pace while continuing her job. The course provided her with valuable insights and practical techniques that she implemented in her projects.

2. Certifications

What They Are: Certifications are formal qualifications that validate your expertise in a specific area. They are often offered by professional organizations or institutions and can boost your credibility and marketability.

Benefits:

- ➤ **Validation:** Demonstrates your proficiency and commitment to your field.
- ➤ **Career Advancement:** Can lead to new job opportunities and higher earning potential.
- ➤ **Professional Growth:** Provides specialized knowledge that can set you apart.

Steps to Utilize:

- ➤ **Select Relevant Certifications:** Choose certifications that align with your career goals and industry demands.
- ➤ **Prepare Thoroughly:** Study and prepare for certification exams through recommended resources and practice tests.
- ➤ **Maintain Credentials:** Stay updated with any continuing education requirements to keep your certification valid.

Example: John, an IT specialist, aimed to advance his career in cybersecurity. He pursued a Certified Information Systems Security Professional (CISSP) certification, which involved intensive study and preparation. Earning this certification not only enhanced his expertise but also opened doors to senior cybersecurity roles.

3. Workshops and Seminars

What They Are: Workshops and seminars provide interactive and hands-on learning experiences. They often focus on specific skills or topics and are conducted by industry experts or practitioners.

Benefits:

> ➤ **Interactive Learning:** Engage directly with instructors and peers.

> ➤ **Networking Opportunities:** Connect with professionals in your field.

> ➤ **Practical Skills:** Gain practical, actionable knowledge that can be applied immediately.

Steps to Utilize:

> ➤ **Find Relevant Events:** Look for workshops and seminars related to your career interests and goals.

> ➤ **Participate Actively:** Engage in discussions, ask questions, and network with other participants.

> **Apply What You Learn:** Implement the skills and knowledge gained in your current role or projects.

Example: Lisa, an HR manager, attended a workshop on effective leadership and team building. The interactive sessions and group exercises helped her develop new strategies for managing her team. She applied these techniques to improve team dynamics and performance, resulting in a more cohesive and productive work environment.

4. Mentorship and Networking

What It Is: Mentorship involves receiving guidance and advice from experienced professionals in your field. Networking includes building relationships with industry peers and leaders.

Benefits:

> **Guidance:** Gain insights and advice from experienced mentors.

> **Opportunities:** Discover new career opportunities through networking connections.

> **Support:** Receive encouragement and feedback on your professional development.

Steps to Utilize:

> **Seek Mentors:** Identify and approach potential mentors who align with your career goals.

> **Network Strategically:** Attend industry events, join professional associations, and engage with peers on platforms like LinkedIn.

> **Maintain Relationships:** Foster ongoing relationships with mentors and network contacts.

Example: David, a financial analyst, sought mentorship from a senior executive in his industry. Through regular meetings and advice, he gained valuable insights into strategic decision-making and career advancement. Networking with industry professionals also led to a new job opportunity that aligned with his career aspirations.

5. Stay Updated with Industry Trends

What It Is: Keeping up with industry trends involves staying informed about the latest developments, technologies, and best practices in your field.

Benefits:

> **Relevance:** Ensure your skills and knowledge remain current.

> **Competitiveness:** Stay ahead of industry changes and position yourself as a knowledgeable professional.

> **Innovation:** Discover new tools and techniques that can enhance your work.

Steps to Utilize:

> **Follow Industry News:** Subscribe to industry journals, newsletters, and blogs.

> **Participate in Webinars:** Attend webinars and online discussions on emerging trends.

> **Engage in Professional Groups:** Join professional organizations and online communities related to your field.

Example: Rachel, a digital marketing professional, subscribed to industry newsletters and attended webinars on new marketing technologies. Staying updated allowed her to integrate the latest tools into her campaigns, leading to more effective marketing strategies and career growth.

Conclusion

Utilizing professional development resources such as online courses, certifications, workshops, and mentorship is crucial for career advancement. By strategically selecting and engaging with these resources, you can enhance your skills, stay current in your field, and position yourself for future opportunities. Embrace these strategies to achieve your career goals and drive your professional growth.

For Freshers

How to Assess and Plan for Career-Related Learning

Navigating Career-Related Learning

As a fresher entering the job market, assessing and planning your career-related learning is crucial for laying a strong foundation for your professional journey. Effective assessment and planning will help you identify the skills and knowledge required for your desired career path and set you up for success. Here's a step-by-step guide to help you assess and plan for career-related learning:

1. Self-Assessment and Career Exploration

Explanation: Start by evaluating your interests, strengths, and career aspirations. Understanding what you enjoy and where your skills lie will help you choose a career path that aligns with your goals and values.

Steps to Take:

- **Identify Interests:** Reflect on subjects or activities that you are passionate about and enjoy.
- **Assess Strengths:** Recognize your strengths and skills through self-assessment tools, feedback from others, or personality tests.
- **Explore Careers:** Research different career options and industries to see which ones match your interests and strengths.

Example: Priya, a recent graduate, was interested in technology and had strong analytical skills. She explored various tech careers, such as software development and data analysis, to determine which path aligned with her interests and skills.

2. Research Industry Requirements and Trends

Explanation: Investigate the skills and qualifications required for your chosen career field. Understanding industry trends will help you identify the competencies in demand and ensure your learning efforts are relevant.

Steps to Take:
- **Job Descriptions:** Review job postings for roles that interest you to identify common skills and qualifications.
- **Industry Reports:** Read industry reports and articles to stay informed about emerging trends and technologies.
- **Professional Networks:** Connect with professionals in your desired field to gain insights into the skills and qualifications they consider essential.

Example: Anil, aspiring to become a digital marketer, researched job descriptions and industry reports to learn about key skills like SEO, content marketing, and social media management. This research guided his learning plan.

3. Set Clear Learning Objectives and Goals

Explanation: Define specific, measurable, achievable, relevant, and time-bound (SMART) learning objectives that align with your career goals. Setting clear objectives will help you stay focused and track your progress.

Steps to Take:
- **SMART Goals:** Create goals such as "Complete a certification in digital marketing within six months" or "Learn basic programming skills within three months."

> **Action Plan:** Develop a plan outlining the steps required to achieve your learning objectives, including resources, timelines, and milestones.

Example: Rina set a goal to learn graphic design software by enrolling in an online course and completing a set number of practice projects within a specified timeframe. Her action plan included weekly study sessions and project deadlines.

4. Choose Appropriate Learning Resources

Explanation: Select learning resources that suit your learning style and goals. Options include online courses, textbooks, workshops, and mentorship programs.

Steps to Take:

> **Online Courses:** Explore platforms like Coursera, Udemy, and edX for relevant courses and certifications.

> **Books and Tutorials:** Find recommended books and tutorials related to your chosen field.

> **Workshops and Webinars:** Attend workshops and webinars to gain practical knowledge and skills.

Example: Raj, aiming to become a software developer, chose an online coding bootcamp that offered hands-on projects and real-world coding challenges. He also used textbooks and online tutorials to supplement his learning.

5. Gain Practical Experience

Explanation: Applying your knowledge through practical experience is essential for reinforcing what you've learned and demonstrating your skills to potential employers.

Steps to Take:

- **Internships:** Seek internships or volunteer opportunities in your field to gain hands-on experience.
- **Projects:** Work on personal or freelance projects to build a portfolio of your work.
- **Networking:** Connect with industry professionals and seek opportunities for practical experience through their recommendations.

Example: Maya, a recent graduate with a degree in marketing, interned with a local marketing agency. During her internship, she worked on real campaigns, which helped her apply her knowledge and build a strong portfolio.

6. Seek Feedback and Continuous Improvement

Explanation: Regularly seek feedback on your learning progress and performance. Use this feedback to refine your skills and make improvements.

Steps to Take:

- **Feedback:** Request feedback from mentors, instructors, or colleagues on your work and progress.

> **Reflection:** Reflect on the feedback and identify areas for improvement.

> **Adjust Plans:** Modify your learning plan based on feedback and new insights.

Example: John, a fresh graduate in graphic design, sought feedback from his mentor on his portfolio. The constructive criticism helped him make adjustments and enhance the quality of his work, leading to better job prospects.

7. Stay Motivated and Adaptable

Explanation: Maintaining motivation and being adaptable in your learning journey is crucial for overcoming challenges and staying committed to your career goals.

Steps to Take:

- **Set Milestones:** Break down your goals into smaller milestones and celebrate your achievements along the way.
- **Stay Flexible:** Be open to adjusting your learning plan based on new opportunities and changes in your interests or the job market.

Example: Sara, pursuing a career in data science, faced challenges with complex topics. She set short-term milestones and rewarded herself for achieving them. Staying flexible, she adjusted her learning plan based on new developments in the field.

Conclusion

Assessing and planning for career-related learning is essential for freshers to build a successful career. By conducting self-assessment, researching industry trends, setting clear goals, choosing appropriate resources, gaining practical experience, seeking feedback, and staying motivated, you can effectively navigate your career development journey. Embrace these strategies to acquire the skills and knowledge needed for career success and achieve your professional aspirations.

Tips for Building a Strong Foundation Through Early Learning Experiences

Establishing a Strong Foundation

Building a solid foundation through early learning experiences is key to long-term career success. For freshers, this means developing essential skills, gaining practical experience, and cultivating habits that will support continuous growth. Here are some actionable tips to help you build a strong foundation early in your career:

1. Embrace a Learning Mindset

Explanation: Cultivating a mindset that values continuous learning and curiosity sets the stage for ongoing personal and professional development. Embrace every opportunity as a chance to learn and grow.

Tips:

- **Be Open to New Ideas:** Approach new challenges with enthusiasm and a willingness to learn.
- **Seek Feedback:** Actively seek constructive feedback and use it to improve your skills and performance.
- **Reflect Regularly:** Take time to reflect on your experiences and what you've learned from them.

Example: Jake, a recent graduate in engineering, approached every project with a desire to learn. He regularly sought feedback from his mentors and reflected on his experiences, which helped him quickly adapt and improve his skills.

2. Build Practical Experience Early

Explanation: Gaining practical experience through internships, projects, or part-time jobs provides valuable insights into your chosen field and helps you apply theoretical knowledge in real-world situations.

Tips:

- **Pursue Internships:** Look for internships or volunteer opportunities related to your field of interest.
- **Work on Projects:** Take on personal or freelance projects to build a portfolio of your work.

> **Participate in Competitions:** Engage in industry-related competitions to showcase your skills and gain exposure.

Example: Maria, an aspiring graphic designer, took on freelance design projects and participated in design competitions. This hands-on experience allowed her to build a strong portfolio and gain confidence in her abilities.

3. Develop Essential Soft Skills

Explanation: Soft skills, such as communication, teamwork, and problem-solving, are crucial for career success and often complement technical skills. Focus on developing these skills to enhance your overall effectiveness in the workplace.

Tips:

> **Practice Communication:** Improve your verbal and written communication skills through presentations, writing exercises, and discussions.

> **Enhance Teamwork:** Participate in group activities or team-based projects to develop collaboration skills.

> **Solve Problems Creatively:** Approach problems with creative solutions and practice critical thinking.

Example: Alex, a fresh graduate in business management, joined a student organization where he worked on team projects and organized events. This experience helped him develop strong communication and teamwork skills that he later applied in his professional role.

4. Build a Strong Professional Network

Explanation: Establishing a professional network early on can provide support, guidance, and opportunities throughout your career. Networking with industry professionals can offer valuable insights and connections.

Tips:

> - **Attend Industry Events:** Participate in conferences, seminars, and networking events to meet professionals in your field.
>
> - **Join Professional Associations:** Become a member of relevant professional organizations or groups.
>
> - **Leverage Social Media:** Use platforms like LinkedIn to connect with industry experts and peers.

Example: Priya, a recent graduate in marketing, attended industry conferences and joined marketing associations. Through these connections, she gained insights from professionals and secured a valuable internship opportunity.

5. Focus on Lifelong Learning Habits

Explanation: Developing habits that support lifelong learning will ensure that you continue to grow and adapt throughout your career. These habits will help you stay current and responsive to industry changes.

Tips:

- **Set Learning Goals:** Regularly set goals for acquiring new skills or knowledge.
- **Read Regularly:** Stay updated with industry news, books, and articles.
- **Take Online Courses:** Continuously enroll in online courses or webinars to expand your knowledge.

Example: John, a fresh graduate in finance, made it a habit to read financial news and take online courses related to emerging trends in the industry. This commitment to learning kept him informed and prepared for career advancements.

6. Seek Mentorship and Guidance

Explanation: Finding a mentor who can provide guidance, support, and advice can be invaluable for your career development. A mentor can offer insights based on their experience and help you navigate your career path.

Tips:

- **Identify Potential Mentors:** Look for experienced professionals in your field who can offer valuable advice.
- **Build Relationships:** Approach potential mentors with a clear request for guidance and be open to their feedback.

> **Be Proactive:** Take the initiative to schedule regular meetings and discussions with your mentor.

Example: Lisa, an aspiring software developer, sought mentorship from a senior developer in her company. The mentor provided guidance on career decisions, coding practices, and networking opportunities, which greatly influenced her career growth.

7. Cultivate Resilience and Adaptability

Explanation: Resilience and adaptability are essential qualities that will help you overcome challenges and thrive in a dynamic work environment. Building these traits will support your career development and long-term success.

Tips:

> **Embrace Challenges:** View challenges as opportunities for growth and learning.

> **Stay Flexible:** Be open to changes and adapt to new situations or roles.

> **Learn from Setbacks:** Use setbacks as learning experiences to improve and move forward.

Example: Raj, a fresh graduate in data science, faced challenges during his first job when adapting to new tools and technologies. By staying resilient and open to learning, he quickly adapted and excelled in his role.

Conclusion

Building a strong foundation through early learning experiences is crucial for career success. By embracing a learning mindset, gaining practical experience, developing soft skills, building a professional network, focusing on lifelong learning, seeking mentorship, and cultivating resilience, you can establish a solid base for your career. Implement these tips to set yourself up for a successful and fulfilling professional journey.

Chapter 3
Exploring Learning Methods

Formal Education

Advantages of Traditional Degrees and Certifications

Traditional Degrees and Certifications: Key Advantages

Formal education, encompassing traditional degrees and certifications, provides structured learning and recognized qualifications that are highly valued across industries. Here are the primary advantages of pursuing these educational paths:

1. Comprehensive and Structured Learning

Explanation: Traditional degrees and certifications offer a structured approach to learning, ensuring that you acquire a broad and deep understanding of your chosen field.

Advantages:

> - **Organized Curriculum:** Degrees and certifications are designed with a clear curriculum that covers essential concepts and advanced topics in a logical sequence.

- ➤ **Expert Instruction:** Courses are taught by qualified instructors who are experts in their fields, providing high-quality education.
- ➤ **Well-Defined Path:** Provides a roadmap for learning, including milestones and assessments to gauge progress.

Example: Alex pursued a Bachelor's degree in Mechanical Engineering. The structured curriculum included core courses in thermodynamics, fluid mechanics, and materials science, which gave him a comprehensive understanding of engineering principles and prepared him for complex real-world applications.

2. Recognized Credentials

Explanation: Traditional degrees and certifications are widely recognized and respected by employers and professional organizations, serving as official proof of your knowledge and skills.

Advantages:

- ➤ **Industry Standard:** Degrees and certifications often meet industry standards and are prerequisites for many professional roles.
- ➤ **Professional Validation:** Credentials validate your expertise and dedication to your profession, enhancing your credibility.
- ➤ **Career Opportunities:** Having a recognized qualification can open doors to job opportunities and career advancement.

Example: Sarah earned a Certified Financial Planner (CFP) designation, which is highly regarded in the finance industry. This certification helped her secure a position at a top financial planning firm and advance her career.

3. Networking and Professional Connections

Explanation: Formal education provides opportunities to connect with peers, instructors, and industry professionals, which can be valuable for career growth.

Advantages:

> - **Peer Networking:** Build relationships with fellow students who can become future colleagues or collaborators.
>
> - **Instructor Connections:** Develop connections with instructors who can offer mentorship and career advice.
>
> - **Industry Events:** Participate in university-organized events, guest lectures, and networking opportunities.

Example: Maya, while pursuing her MBA, networked with classmates and professors. These connections led to job referrals and industry insights, which significantly benefited her career trajectory.

4. Access to Resources and Support

Explanation: Educational institutions often provide access to various resources and support services that enhance the learning experience and help students succeed.

Advantages:

- ➢ **Research Facilities:** Access to extensive libraries, research databases, and academic resources.
- ➢ **Career Services:** Support with job placement, internships, resume writing, and interview preparation.
- ➢ **Academic Support:** Assistance with coursework, tutoring, and academic counseling.

Example: Raj's university provided a career services center that helped him with resume writing and interview coaching. These resources were instrumental in securing his first job after graduation.

5. Pathway to Advanced Roles

Explanation: Degrees and certifications often serve as prerequisites for advanced career opportunities and specialization, providing a pathway to higher-level positions.

Advantages:

- ➢ **Qualifications for Advancement:** Certain roles or promotions may require advanced degrees or specialized certifications.
- ➢ **Professional Development:** Credentials can lead to further specialization or leadership roles.
- ➢ **Competitive Edge:** Qualifications can give you a competitive advantage in the job market.

Example: Priya, with a Master's degree in Data Science, qualified for roles such as Data Scientist and Analytics Manager, which required advanced knowledge and skills beyond a bachelor's degree.

6. Validation of Skills and Knowledge

Explanation: Formal education involves structured assessments that validate your understanding and abilities through exams, projects, and practical evaluations.

Advantages:

- **Objective Measurement:** Assessments provide an objective measure of your knowledge and skills.
- **Feedback Mechanism:** Regular feedback helps you identify strengths and areas for improvement.
- **Certification Achievement:** Successful completion of coursework and exams leads to formal certification or degree.

Example: John completed a series of exams and practical projects as part of his IT certification program. The assessments validated his skills and provided him with a recognized certification that enhanced his job prospects.

7. Long-Term Benefits

Explanation: The benefits of formal education often extend beyond immediate career opportunities, offering long-term value through ongoing professional growth and personal development.

Advantages:

> **Foundation for Lifelong Learning:** Provides a strong foundation for continued learning and career development.

> **Transferable Skills:** Many skills acquired through formal education are transferable across various roles and industries.

> **Career Flexibility:** Enables you to pivot to different career paths or industries if needed.

Example: Lisa, with a background in engineering, found that her problem-solving and analytical skills were valuable when transitioning to a project management role, showcasing the long-term benefits of her formal education.

Conclusion

Traditional degrees and certifications offer numerous advantages, including structured learning, recognized credentials, networking opportunities, access to resources, pathways to advanced roles, validation of skills, and long-term benefits. These qualifications provide a solid foundation for career success and personal growth, making them a valuable investment in your future. By pursuing formal education, you can gain the knowledge, skills, and recognition needed to achieve your professional and personal goals.

How to Choose the Right Educational Path

Choosing the right educational path is a crucial decision that can significantly impact your career and personal growth. With various options available, it's important to carefully evaluate your goals, interests, and resources to make an informed choice. Here's a step-by-step guide to help you choose the right educational path:

1. Identify Your Goals and Interests

Explanation: Start by understanding your career aspirations and personal interests. This will help you select an educational path that aligns with your long-term objectives and passions.

Steps:

- ➤ **Define Your Career Goals:** Determine what you want to achieve in your career, such as the type of job, industry, or level of responsibility.

- ➤ **Assess Your Interests:** Consider what subjects or fields you are passionate about and enjoy studying.

- ➤ **Evaluate Your Strengths:** Reflect on your skills and strengths to identify areas where you can excel.

Example: If you aspire to become a data scientist and have a strong interest in mathematics and programming, pursuing a degree in Computer Science or Data Science might be a suitable path.

2. Research Educational Options

Explanation: Explore various educational programs and institutions to find the one that best fits your needs. This includes evaluating the curriculum, faculty, and resources offered.

Steps:

> ➢ **Compare Programs:** Look at different degree programs, certifications, and courses related to your field of interest.
>
> ➢ **Evaluate Institutions:** Research the reputation, accreditation, and support services of educational institutions.
>
> ➢ **Review Curriculum:** Examine the course content, structure, and any specializations or electives available.

Example: Researching multiple universities for a Master's program in Business Administration can help you find a program with a strong focus on leadership or entrepreneurship, depending on your career goals.

3. Consider Your Time and Financial Resources

Explanation: Assess the time commitment and financial investment required for each educational path. Choose an option that fits your schedule and budget.

Steps:

> ➢ **Evaluate Duration:** Consider the length of the program and whether you can commit to the time required.

- **Calculate Costs:** Analyze tuition fees, additional expenses, and potential financial aid or scholarships.
- **Balance with Other Responsibilities:** Ensure that the educational path you choose can be balanced with your current work or personal responsibilities.

Example: If you are working full-time and have financial constraints, you might consider part-time or online courses that offer flexibility while fitting within your budget.

4. Seek Advice and Guidance

Explanation: Consulting with mentors, professionals, and academic advisors can provide valuable insights and help you make an informed decision.

Steps:

- **Talk to Professionals:** Speak with individuals who are working in your desired field to understand the qualifications and skills they value.
- **Consult Academic Advisors:** Seek advice from academic advisors or career counselors who can provide guidance based on your goals and interests.
- **Network with Alumni:** Connect with alumni from programs you are considering to gain insights into their experiences and career outcomes.

Example: Consulting with a career counselor at your current job can help you determine whether pursuing an advanced degree or certification will benefit your career progression.

5. Evaluate the Potential for Career Advancement

Explanation: Consider how the educational path will impact your career opportunities and advancement potential. Look for programs that offer relevant skills and credentials in high demand.

Steps:

> - **Assess Job Market Demand:** Research the demand for qualifications in your chosen field and how they align with industry trends.
> - **Review Career Outcomes:** Look at the career paths and success rates of graduates from the programs you are considering.
> - **Check for Industry Recognition:** Ensure that the qualifications are recognized and valued by employers in your industry.

Example: Pursuing a certification in Project Management might open doors to higher-level project management roles and increase your chances of career advancement.

6. Explore Accreditation and Quality

Explanation: Ensure that the educational program you choose is accredited and meets quality standards. Accreditation ensures that the program meets specific academic and professional criteria.

Steps:

- **Check Accreditation:** Verify that the program is accredited by a recognized accrediting body or professional organization.
- **Review Quality Indicators:** Look for indicators of program quality, such as faculty qualifications, research opportunities, and student support services.
- **Read Reviews and Testimonials:** Consider reviews and testimonials from current or former students to gauge the program's quality and effectiveness.

Example: Before enrolling in a certification program for digital marketing, confirm that it is accredited by a reputable organization and has positive reviews from past participants.

7. Plan for Personal Growth and Development

Explanation: Choose an educational path that not only meets your career goals but also supports your personal growth and development. Look for programs that offer opportunities for skill enhancement and personal enrichment.

Steps:

- **Explore Extracurricular Opportunities:** Look for programs that offer extracurricular activities, internships, or projects that can enhance your learning experience.
- **Consider Personal Interests:** Choose a path that aligns with your personal interests and

values, contributing to a fulfilling educational experience.

> **Set Personal Development Goals:** Identify goals for personal growth that you want to achieve through your educational journey.

Example: Enrolling in a leadership development program as part of your MBA can help you build essential leadership skills and contribute to both your career and personal growth.

Conclusion

Choosing the right educational path involves careful consideration of your goals, interests, resources, and the quality of the programs available. By identifying your objectives, researching options, assessing time and financial commitments, seeking advice, evaluating career advancement potential, ensuring accreditation and quality, and planning for personal growth, you can make an informed decision that aligns with your aspirations. Taking these steps will help you select an educational path that supports your long-term success and fulfillment.

Online Learning and Courses

Overview of Popular Online Learning Platforms

Online Learning Platforms: A Comprehensive Overview

Online learning has become increasingly popular, offering flexible and accessible educational opportunities for learners worldwide. Here's an overview of some of the most popular online learning platforms, each catering to different needs and preferences:

1. Coursera

Explanation: Coursera partners with universities and organizations to offer a wide range of online courses, specializations, and degrees. The platform provides high-quality education from renowned institutions.

Features:

> - **Course Variety:** Offers courses in various fields including technology, business, arts, and science.
>
> - **Degrees and Certifications:** Provides access to full degree programs and professional certifications.
>
> - **Flexible Learning:** Allows learners to study at their own pace with options for free and paid courses.

Example: Sarah completed a data science specialization on Coursera, which included courses from top universities. The certification she earned helped her advance her career as a data analyst.

2. Udemy

Explanation: Udemy is a popular platform that offers a vast library of courses created by experts and industry professionals. It focuses on practical skills and professional development.

Features:

> **Diverse Course Catalog:** Covers a wide range of topics including programming, design, marketing, and personal development.

> **One-Time Purchase:** Courses are typically purchased individually, often with lifetime access.

> **User Reviews:** Provides reviews and ratings from other learners to help choose the best courses.

Example: John learned web development through a Udemy course, which included hands-on projects and real-world examples. The skills he gained helped him launch his own freelance web development business.

3. edX

Explanation: edX, founded by Harvard and MIT, offers high-quality courses, MicroMasters programs, and professional certificates from leading universities and institutions.

Features:

> **Academic Rigor:** Courses are designed and taught by university professors and industry experts.

> **Professional Credentials:** Provides options for professional certificates and MicroMasters programs.

> **Flexible Enrollment:** Offers both free and paid courses with various start dates and schedules.

Example: Maria completed a MicroMasters program in artificial intelligence on edX, which provided her with advanced knowledge and credentials to pursue a role in AI research.

4. LinkedIn Learning

Explanation: LinkedIn Learning offers courses designed to enhance professional skills and career development. It integrates with LinkedIn profiles to showcase completed courses and certifications.

Features:

> - **Skill-Based Courses:** Focuses on practical skills in areas such as business, technology, and creative fields.
>
> - **Professional Development:** Offers courses tailored to career growth and industry trends.
>
> - **Integration with LinkedIn:** Completed courses and certifications are displayed on LinkedIn profiles.

Example: Alex took several courses on LinkedIn Learning to improve his project management skills. The new skills and certifications helped him secure a promotion at his company.

5. Khan Academy

Explanation: Khan Academy provides free educational resources and courses for students of all ages. It focuses on foundational subjects and offers a wide range of interactive learning materials.

Features:

- **Free Access:** All courses and resources are available for free, making it accessible to everyone.

- **Interactive Learning:** Includes video lessons, practice exercises, and progress tracking.

- **K-12 and Beyond:** Covers subjects from elementary school through college-level courses.

Example: Emily used Khan Academy to supplement her high school math education, finding the interactive exercises and video lessons helpful in understanding complex concepts.

6. Skillshare

Explanation: Skillshare offers a variety of creative and practical courses, focusing on hands-on projects and skills development in areas like design, photography, and writing.

Features:

- **Project-Based Learning:** Emphasizes practical skills and project-based assignments.

- **Community Engagement:** Includes discussions and feedback from instructors and peers.

- **Subscription Model:** Provides access to all courses with a subscription plan.

Example: Liam improved his graphic design skills through a Skillshare course that included real-world projects and feedback from industry professionals.

7. FutureLearn

Explanation: FutureLearn provides a diverse range of courses from universities and organizations, focusing on professional and personal development.

Features:

> - **Courses and Degrees:** Offers short courses, Microcredentials, and full degree programs.
> - **Collaborative Learning:** Includes discussion forums and group activities.
> - **Flexible Study:** Provides options for free and paid courses with various learning schedules.

Example: Chloe completed a FutureLearn course on digital marketing, which included interactive assignments and peer feedback, enhancing her knowledge and skills in the field.

8. Pluralsight

Explanation: Pluralsight focuses on technology and IT skills, offering courses on topics such as software development, cloud computing, and cybersecurity.

Features:

> - **Tech-Focused:** Specializes in courses for IT professionals and technology enthusiasts.
> - **Skill Assessments:** Provides assessments and learning paths to track progress and skill development.
> - **Expert Instructors:** Courses are taught by industry experts and professionals.

Example: Raj used Pluralsight to gain advanced knowledge in cloud computing, which helped him earn a cloud architect certification and advance his career.

Conclusion

Each online learning platform offers unique features and benefits, catering to different learning styles and needs. By exploring these platforms, you can find the one that best aligns with your educational goals and career aspirations. Whether you're looking to gain new skills, advance your career, or explore new interests, online learning provides flexible and accessible opportunities to achieve your objectives.

Tips for Selecting High-Quality Online Courses and Programs

Selecting high-quality online courses and programs is essential for ensuring that you gain valuable knowledge and skills effectively. Here are some tips to help you choose the best online learning opportunities:

1. Check Course Reviews and Ratings

Explanation: Reviews and ratings from previous learners provide insights into the course's quality and effectiveness. They can help you gauge whether the course meets your expectations and learning goals.

Tips:
- ➤ **Read Detailed Reviews:** Look for detailed feedback from learners about the course content, instructor quality, and overall experience.

- ➤ **Consider Overall Ratings:** Higher ratings generally indicate better quality, but read individual comments for a more nuanced understanding.

- ➤ **Look for Verified Reviews:** Prioritize reviews on reputable platforms where feedback is verified and authentic.

Example: Before enrolling in a programming course, read reviews on platforms like Udemy or Coursera to see if past students found the course engaging and useful for their career goals.

2. Evaluate Instructor Qualifications

Explanation: The expertise and background of the instructor play a significant role in the quality of the course. Instructors with relevant experience and credentials are more likely to provide valuable learning experiences.

Tips:

- ➤ **Review Instructor Profiles:** Check the instructor's qualifications, experience, and professional background.

- ➤ **Look for Industry Experience:** Instructors with practical experience in the field can provide real-world insights and examples.

- ➤ **Assess Teaching Style:** Watch introductory videos or sample lessons to assess the instructor's teaching style and effectiveness.

Example: If you're considering a course on data science, ensure that the instructor has industry experience and relevant academic qualifications, such as a PhD or significant work in the field.

3. Examine Course Content and Structure

Explanation: A well-structured course with clear objectives and comprehensive content is crucial for effective learning. Review the course syllabus to ensure it covers the topics you want to learn and is organized logically.

Tips:

- ➤ **Review the Syllabus:** Check the course outline to ensure it covers relevant topics and includes practical exercises or projects.

- ➤ **Assess Learning Outcomes:** Look for clear learning objectives and outcomes to understand what you will gain from the course.

- ➤ **Check for Updates:** Ensure the course content is up-to-date with current industry trends and practices.

Example: For a course on digital marketing, make sure the syllabus includes current trends like social media strategies and SEO practices, not just outdated methods.

4. Verify Accreditation and Certification

Explanation: Accreditation and certification from reputable institutions add credibility to the course and can be beneficial for your career advancement. Ensure that the course offers recognized credentials.

Tips:

- **Check Accreditation:** Verify if the course or program is accredited by a reputable organization or educational institution.
- **Look for Recognized Certifications:** Ensure that the certification you earn is recognized and valued by employers in your industry.
- **Research Institutional Partnerships:** Courses offered in partnership with well-known universities or organizations often have higher credibility.

Example: If you're pursuing a project management course, check if it provides a certification recognized by organizations like PMI (Project Management Institute).

5. Evaluate Flexibility and Accessibility

Explanation: Flexibility and accessibility are important for balancing your learning with other responsibilities. Ensure that the course format and schedule fit your needs.

Tips:

- **Check Course Format:** Look for courses that offer flexible learning options, such as on-demand videos, self-paced modules, or live sessions.
- **Assess Accessibility:** Ensure the course platform is accessible on various devices and provides necessary resources like subtitles or additional materials.

> **Consider Time Commitment:** Choose courses that fit your schedule and allow you to manage your time effectively.

Example: If you're working full-time, opt for a course with on-demand content that you can access at your convenience, rather than one with fixed class times.

6. Look for Interactive and Engaging Elements

Explanation: Interactive elements enhance learning by providing hands-on experience and opportunities for engagement. Courses with interactive features often lead to a better understanding of the material.

Tips:

> **Check for Hands-On Projects:** Look for courses that include practical projects, case studies, or real-world applications.

> **Review Discussion Forums:** Ensure the course includes discussion forums or peer interaction for collaborative learning and feedback.

> **Evaluate Quizzes and Assessments:** Interactive quizzes and assessments help reinforce learning and track progress.

Example: A course on graphic design with interactive projects and feedback from peers can provide a more practical and engaging learning experience compared to a lecture-based course.

7. Compare Costs and Value

Explanation: Consider the cost of the course relative to the value it provides. Look for courses that offer a good balance between affordability and the quality of education.

Tips:

- **Compare Prices:** Compare the costs of similar courses and check if they offer any financial aid or discounts.
- **Evaluate Included Resources:** Consider the additional resources provided, such as access to software, learning materials, or mentorship.
- **Assess Return on Investment:** Think about how the course will contribute to your career goals and if it justifies the investment.

Example: A higher-priced course with extensive resources and certification may offer better value than a cheaper course with limited content and no credential.

8. Look for Trial or Sample Lessons

Explanation: Trial or sample lessons provide a preview of the course content and teaching style, helping you decide if it meets your expectations before committing.

Tips:

- **Access Free Previews:** Many platforms offer free trial lessons or previews of course content.
- **Evaluate Sample Content:** Use sample lessons to assess the quality of instruction and the relevance of the material.
- **Assess Usability:** Ensure that the course platform is user-friendly and that the sample lessons are engaging and informative.

Example: Before enrolling in a coding bootcamp, watch the introductory videos or sample lessons to ensure the teaching style and content are aligned with your learning preferences.

Conclusion

Choosing high-quality online courses and programs requires careful consideration of reviews, instructor qualifications, course content, accreditation, flexibility, interactive elements, costs, and sample lessons. By following these tips, you can select educational opportunities that provide valuable knowledge and skills, supporting your personal and professional growth effectively.

Self-Directed Learning

Techniques for Self-Study and Independent Learning

Self directed learning empowers individuals to take control of their own educational journey, fostering independence and personal growth. Here are effective techniques for self-study and independent learning that can help you succeed:

1. Set Clear Learning Goals

Explanation: Establishing specific and achievable goals provides direction and motivation for your self-directed learning efforts. Clearly defined objectives help you stay focused and track your progress.

Techniques:

➢ **Define Objectives:** Identify what you want to achieve with your learning. This could be mastering a new skill, understanding a concept, or completing a project.

➢ **Break Down Goals:** Divide larger goals into smaller, manageable tasks or milestones.

➢ **Set Deadlines:** Assign deadlines to each task to maintain accountability and momentum.

Example: If you want to learn Python programming, set goals like completing an introductory course within a month and building a simple project by the end of two months.

2. Create a Structured Study Plan

Explanation: A well-organized study plan helps manage your time effectively and ensures that you cover all necessary material systematically.

Techniques:

➢ **Develop a Schedule:** Allocate specific times for study sessions and stick to the schedule.

➢ **Organize Content:** Arrange learning materials in a logical sequence, starting with foundational concepts and progressing to advanced topics.

➢ **Include Breaks:** Incorporate breaks and downtime to avoid burnout and enhance retention.

Example: Create a weekly study plan for learning digital marketing, including time for reading articles, watching videos, and practicing skills, with regular breaks to review and reflect.

3. Utilize Various Learning Resources

Explanation: Leveraging diverse resources can enrich your learning experience and provide multiple perspectives on the subject matter.

Techniques:

- **Explore Different Media:** Use a combination of books, online courses, videos, podcasts, and articles to gain a comprehensive understanding.

- **Engage with Interactive Tools:** Incorporate quizzes, simulations, and interactive exercises to reinforce learning.

- **Join Learning Communities:** Participate in online forums, discussion groups, or study groups to connect with others and exchange knowledge.

Example: While learning about financial management, read relevant books, watch instructional videos, listen to finance podcasts, and use budgeting apps to apply concepts practically.

4. Practice Active Learning

Explanation: Active learning techniques involve engaging directly with the material, which enhances understanding and retention.

Techniques:

- **Summarize Information:** Regularly summarize what you've learned in your own words to reinforce comprehension.

- **Teach Others:** Explaining concepts to others can deepen your understanding and reveal any gaps in knowledge.

- **Apply Knowledge:** Work on real-world projects or problems to apply what you've learned in practical situations.

Example: After studying a chapter on machine learning algorithms, write a blog post summarizing key points, teach a friend about the algorithms, and build a small machine learning model to apply the concepts.

5. Monitor Your Progress

Explanation: Regularly assessing your progress helps you stay on track, identify areas for improvement, and adjust your learning strategies as needed.

Techniques:

- **Track Milestones:** Record your achievements and progress towards your goals.

- **Evaluate Understanding:** Use self-assessment quizzes or practice tests to gauge your understanding of the material.

- **Reflect on Learning:** Periodically review what you've learned and adjust your study plan based on your reflections.

Example: Use a journal or digital tool to track your progress in learning web development, noting completed projects, areas of improvement, and feedback received.

6. Develop Self-Discipline and Motivation

Explanation: Maintaining self-discipline and motivation is crucial for staying committed to self-directed learning, especially when faced with distractions or challenges.

Techniques:

- ➢ **Set Up a Study Environment:** Create a dedicated and distraction-free space for studying.
- ➢ **Use Motivation Techniques:** Employ techniques such as setting rewards for achieving milestones or visualizing your success.
- ➢ **Stay Accountable:** Share your learning goals with a friend or mentor who can provide support and encouragement.

Example: If you're learning graphic design, set up a quiet workspace, reward yourself with a small treat after completing a design project, and share your progress with a friend who can offer feedback and encouragement.

7. Seek Feedback and Reflect

Explanation: Feedback from others and self-reflection helps improve your learning process and ensure that you're on the right track.

Techniques:

- ➤ **Ask for Feedback:** Share your work or progress with peers, mentors, or experts to receive constructive feedback.
- ➤ **Reflect on Learning:** Regularly reflect on what's working well and what could be improved in your learning approach.
- ➤ **Adjust Strategies:** Based on feedback and reflection, make adjustments to your study plan or methods to enhance effectiveness.

Example: After completing a coding project, seek feedback from a developer community or mentor, reflect on the feedback, and adjust your learning approach to address any identified areas for improvement.

8. Stay Curious and Open-Minded

Explanation: Cultivating curiosity and an open mind fosters a lifelong love of learning and encourages exploration beyond the basics.

Techniques:

- ➤ **Explore New Topics:** Regularly seek out new subjects or areas of interest related to your field.
- ➤ **Stay Informed:** Keep up with current trends, advancements, and innovations in your area of study.
- ➤ **Embrace Challenges:** View challenges as opportunities for growth and learning.

Example: While learning about artificial intelligence, explore related fields such as ethics in AI or emerging technologies to broaden your understanding and stay engaged.

Conclusion

Self-directed learning requires effective planning, diverse resources, active engagement, and self-motivation. By setting clear goals, creating structured plans, using various resources, practicing actively, monitoring progress, developing discipline, seeking feedback, and staying curious, you can successfully navigate your independent learning journey. Embrace these techniques to enhance your self-study efforts and achieve your educational and personal growth objectives.

Using Books, Podcasts, and Other Resources Effectively

Effective self-directed learning involves leveraging various resources to gain knowledge and skills independently. Here's how you can make the most of books, podcasts, and other resources:

1. Maximizing the Use of Books

Explanation: Books offer in-depth knowledge and can be a foundational resource for self-directed learning. Using them effectively requires strategic selection and engagement.

Techniques:

- ➤ **Choose Relevant Books:** Select books that align with your learning goals and interests. Look for recommendations from experts or trusted sources in your field.

- ➤ **Read Actively:** Take notes, highlight key points, and summarize chapters to reinforce understanding.

- ➤ **Apply Learnings:** Implement concepts from books in real-world scenarios or projects to deepen your comprehension.

Example: If you're learning about leadership, choose highly recommended books on leadership principles, such as *"Leaders Eat Last"* by Simon Sinek. Actively take notes on leadership strategies and apply them in your workplace to test their effectiveness.

2. Leveraging Podcasts for Learning

Explanation: Podcasts provide accessible and often conversational insights on various topics. They can be a valuable supplement to more structured learning methods.

Techniques:

- ➤ **Select Quality Podcasts:** Choose podcasts hosted by experts or featuring interviews with industry leaders. Look for those with high ratings and positive reviews.

- ➤ **Listen Actively:** Engage with the content by taking notes, reflecting on key takeaways, and considering how the information applies to your learning goals.

➢ **Follow Up:** Explore additional resources or episodes related to the podcast topics to further your understanding.

Example: For learning about entrepreneurship, listen to podcasts like *"How I Built This"* by Guy Raz. Take notes on the business strategies discussed and research further into topics that pique your interest.

3. Utilizing Online Articles and Blogs

Explanation: Online articles and blogs offer current, niche, and practical information. They are often updated regularly and can provide fresh perspectives and insights.

Techniques:

➢ **Curate Your Sources:** Follow reputable websites and blogs in your area of interest. Subscribe to newsletters or RSS feeds to stay updated.

➢ **Read Critically:** Assess the credibility of the source and cross-reference information with other resources to ensure accuracy.

➢ **Apply and Share:** Use insights gained from articles and blogs to inform your projects and share valuable information with peers or in your professional network.

Example: If you're interested in digital marketing trends, follow industry blogs like *Moz Blog* or *Neil*

Patel's Blog. Use the latest strategies discussed in these blogs to refine your marketing campaigns.

4. Exploring Online Courses and Webinars

Explanation: Online courses and webinars offer structured learning experiences and can provide interactive elements that enhance understanding.

Techniques:

- ➤ **Choose Courses Wisely:** Select courses that have good reviews, are taught by experts, and align with your learning objectives.

- ➤ **Participate Actively:** Engage with course materials, complete assignments, and participate in discussions or Q&A sessions.

- ➤ **Apply Knowledge:** Implement what you learn in real-world projects or scenarios to solidify your understanding.

Example: Enroll in a course on data visualization through platforms like Coursera or edX. Actively participate in the course, complete projects, and use the skills acquired to analyze and present data at work.

5. Engaging with Educational Videos and Tutorials

Explanation: Educational videos and tutorials provide visual and auditory learning opportunities, making complex topics easier to understand.

Techniques:

- ➤ **Select High-Quality Content:** Choose videos from reputable creators or organizations that offer clear, well-structured content.

- ➤ **Watch Actively:** Take notes during videos, pause and replay segments to reinforce understanding, and follow along with any provided exercises.

- ➤ **Practice Skills:** Apply the techniques or concepts demonstrated in the videos to practical tasks or projects.

Example: For learning a new programming language, watch tutorial series on YouTube or educational platforms like Khan Academy. Practice coding alongside the tutorial to gain hands-on experience.

6. Using Interactive Tools and Apps

Explanation: Interactive tools and apps can provide engaging and practical ways to reinforce learning through hands-on activities and real-time feedback.

Techniques:

- ➤ **Select Relevant Tools:** Choose apps or tools that match your learning objectives, such as language learning apps or coding practice platforms.

- ➤ **Engage Regularly:** Use the tools consistently to practice and apply your skills. Set goals and track your progress within the app.

> **Supplement Learning:** Combine app-based learning with other resources to gain a well-rounded understanding.

Example: Use a language learning app like Duolingo to practice a new language daily. Complement this with language books and conversation practice to enhance your proficiency.

7. Participating in Online Forums and Communities

Explanation: Online forums and communities provide opportunities for discussion, networking, and knowledge sharing with others interested in similar topics.

Techniques:

> **Join Relevant Communities:** Participate in forums or groups related to your learning goals, such as Reddit's subreddits or LinkedIn groups.

> **Engage Actively:** Ask questions, share insights, and contribute to discussions to gain and offer knowledge.

> **Network and Collaborate:** Connect with others in the community for collaborative learning and feedback.

Example: Join a forum for graphic design enthusiasts to discuss trends, get feedback on your work, and learn from others' experiences.

8. Creating a Personal Learning Resource Library

Explanation: Building a personal library of resources allows you to curate and organize materials that are most valuable to your learning journey.

Techniques:

- **Organize Resources:** Use digital tools like Evernote or Zotero to store and categorize books, articles, videos, and notes.
- **Regularly Update:** Add new resources and remove outdated ones to keep your library relevant and useful.
- **Review and Reflect:** Periodically review your library to reflect on what you've learned and identify areas for further exploration.

Example: Create a digital library for learning project management, including e-books, course materials, and notes. Use this library to track your progress and access resources as needed.

Conclusion

Effectively using books, podcasts, online articles, courses, videos, interactive tools, forums, and personal libraries can enhance your self-directed learning experience. By strategically selecting and engaging with these resources, you can deepen your understanding, apply new skills, and achieve your educational and personal growth goals. Embrace these techniques to maximize the benefits of self-directed learning and advance your knowledge in your chosen fields.

Experiential Learning

Learning Through Practical Experience and Real-World Applications

Experiential learning emphasizes gaining knowledge and skills through direct experience and application. This approach often leads to deeper understanding and retention. Here's how you can effectively engage in experiential learning:

1. Hands-On Projects

Explanation: Working on practical projects provides real-world experience and allows you to apply theoretical knowledge. It helps solidify learning through tangible outcomes.

Techniques:

- **Choose Relevant Projects:** Select projects that align with your learning goals and interests. These projects should challenge you and provide opportunities to apply new skills.

- **Plan and Execute:** Outline the steps required for the project, set milestones, and execute the plan. Document your progress and reflect on the results.

- **Iterate and Improve:** Based on your experience, refine your approach and implement improvements for better outcomes.

Example: If you're learning web development, build a personal website or a web application. As you work through the project, you'll apply coding concepts, debug issues, and create a functional end product.

2. Internships and Work Experience

Explanation: Internships and work experiences offer valuable insights into professional environments and practices. They provide opportunities to apply classroom knowledge in real-world settings.

Techniques:

- ➤ **Seek Relevant Opportunities:** Look for internships, part-time jobs, or volunteer positions related to your field of interest.

- ➤ **Set Learning Goals:** Define what you want to achieve from the experience, such as gaining specific skills or understanding industry practices.

- ➤ **Reflect and Document:** Regularly reflect on your experiences, document your learnings, and assess how they align with your career goals.

Example: An aspiring marketer might intern at a digital marketing agency to gain hands-on experience with campaign management, content creation, and data analysis.

3. Simulations and Role-Playing

Explanation: Simulations and role-playing exercises provide a controlled environment to practice and apply skills in realistic scenarios.

Techniques:

- ➢ **Participate in Simulations:** Engage in simulations related to your field, such as business strategy games or virtual labs.

- ➢ **Role-Play Scenarios:** Take part in role-playing exercises to practice skills like negotiation, public speaking, or problem-solving.

- ➢ **Debrief and Reflect:** After the simulation or role-play, review your performance, gather feedback, and reflect on areas for improvement.

Example: A student learning conflict resolution might participate in role-playing exercises to practice negotiating solutions in various scenarios, enhancing their ability to handle real-world conflicts.

4. Case Studies and Problem Solving

Explanation: Analyzing case studies and solving real-world problems helps you apply theoretical knowledge to practical situations, enhancing critical thinking and problem-solving skills.

Techniques:

- ➢ **Study Case Studies:** Review and analyze case studies relevant to your field. Identify key issues, solutions, and outcomes.

- ➢ **Solve Problems:** Work on problem-solving exercises or case studies related to your area of interest. Develop and implement solutions based on your analysis.

> **Discuss and Collaborate:** Share your findings and solutions with peers or mentors for feedback and discussion.

Example: In a business management course, analyze a case study of a company facing financial challenges. Develop a strategic plan to address the issues and present your solution to the class.

5. Real-World Applications

Explanation: Applying what you've learned to real-world situations reinforces knowledge and demonstrates practical utility.

Techniques:

> **Identify Opportunities:** Look for opportunities to apply new skills or knowledge in everyday situations or professional tasks.

> **Implement Solutions:** Use your skills to solve real problems or create value in practical settings.

> **Evaluate Impact:** Assess the effectiveness of your application and gather feedback to refine your approach.

Example: If you've learned about project management techniques, apply them to organize a community event. Use project planning tools, manage timelines, and coordinate tasks to ensure a successful event.

6. Networking and Mentorship

Explanation: Engaging with professionals and mentors in your field provides insights, guidance, and practical advice based on their experiences.

Techniques:

> - **Build Connections:** Network with industry professionals through events, online forums, and social media platforms.
>
> - **Seek Mentorship:** Find a mentor who can provide personalized guidance, feedback, and support in your learning journey.
>
> - **Engage in Discussions:** Participate in industry discussions, ask questions, and seek advice to gain practical insights.

Example: Connect with experienced data scientists through LinkedIn or professional groups. Seek mentorship to gain insights into industry best practices and receive feedback on your projects.

7. Continuous Feedback and Improvement

Explanation: Regular feedback and iterative improvement help refine your skills and knowledge through practical experience.

Techniques:

> - **Seek Feedback:** Regularly request feedback from peers, mentors, or supervisors on your work or projects.

- ➤ **Reflect on Feedback:** Analyze feedback to identify areas for improvement and adjust your approach accordingly.
- ➤ **Implement Improvements:** Apply feedback to enhance your skills, processes, or outcomes in future experiences.

Example: After completing a design project, solicit feedback from clients or colleagues. Use their insights to improve your design skills and refine your approach for future projects.

8. Participatory Learning

Explanation: Engaging in collaborative and participatory learning experiences allows you to learn from others and contribute your own insights.

Techniques:
- ➤ **Join Study Groups:** Participate in or form study groups to discuss topics, share knowledge, and work on collaborative projects.
- ➤ **Attend Workshops:** Engage in workshops or hands-on sessions where you can actively participate and learn from instructors and peers.
- ➤ **Contribute to Discussions:** Share your knowledge and experiences in group settings to foster mutual learning and collaboration.

Example: Join a study group focused on artificial intelligence. Collaborate on projects, share insights, and work together to solve problems and deepen your understanding of AI concepts.

Conclusion

Experiential learning involves applying knowledge through practical experiences, enhancing understanding, and developing skills. By engaging in hands-on projects, internships, simulations, case studies, real-world applications, networking, feedback, and participatory learning, you can gain valuable insights and achieve meaningful growth. Embrace these techniques to enrich your self-directed learning journey and achieve your personal and professional goals.

Examples of How Hands-On Experiences Can Enhance Learning

Experiential learning is powerful because it bridges the gap between theoretical knowledge and practical application. Here are some compelling examples illustrating how hands-on experiences can significantly enhance learning:

1. Coding Bootcamps

Explanation: Coding bootcamps are intensive programs designed to teach programming through practical, hands-on projects. Participants learn by doing, which helps solidify coding concepts and skills.

Example: In a coding bootcamp, learners work on real-world projects like building a web application or developing a mobile app. By tackling these projects, they apply their coding knowledge, troubleshoot issues, and refine their skills in a practical context. The hands-on experience accelerates learning and prepares them for real-world programming challenges.

2. Business Simulations

Explanation: Business simulations provide a controlled environment where individuals can experience running a business, making decisions, and handling various scenarios without real-world risks.

Example: In a business simulation game, participants manage a virtual company, making decisions on marketing, production, and finance. They observe the outcomes of their decisions, learn about market dynamics, and develop strategic thinking skills. The practical experience of managing a simulated business helps them understand complex business concepts and their implications.

3. Laboratory Experiments

Explanation: Laboratory experiments offer hands-on experience in scientific research and experimentation, allowing learners to apply theoretical knowledge to practical tasks.

Example: In a chemistry lab, students conduct experiments to test chemical reactions, measure properties, and analyze results. By performing these experiments, they learn about scientific methods, data analysis, and problem-solving. The hands-on nature of lab work reinforces theoretical concepts and enhances their understanding of scientific principles.

4. Internship Projects

Explanation: Internships provide real-world work experience, allowing individuals to apply their academic knowledge in a professional setting and gain practical skills.

Example: An intern at a marketing firm may work on actual marketing campaigns, conduct market research, and analyze campaign performance. This hands-on experience helps them understand industry practices, develop professional skills, and gain insights into the workings of a real marketing department. It also offers opportunities for networking and career development.

5. Design Thinking Workshops

Explanation: Design thinking workshops use hands-on activities to solve problems creatively and develop innovative solutions through iterative prototyping and feedback.

Example: In a design thinking workshop, participants work in teams to tackle a design challenge, such as creating a new product or service. They engage in brainstorming sessions, build prototypes, and test their ideas with users. This experiential approach fosters creativity, problem-solving, and collaboration, helping them develop practical skills and insights.

6. Community Service Projects

Explanation: Community service projects offer hands-on experiences in addressing social issues and contributing to community well-being. They provide practical applications of skills while making a positive impact.

Example: Volunteers working on a community garden project apply their skills in gardening, project management, and teamwork to create and maintain a community space. This hands-on experience helps them understand the practical aspects of project execution, collaborate with others, and contribute to community development.

7. Simulation-Based Training

Explanation: Simulation-based training uses interactive scenarios to teach skills and decision-making in a realistic environment. It allows learners to practice and refine their abilities in a risk-free setting.

Example: In a medical simulation, healthcare professionals practice surgical procedures using advanced simulators that mimic real-life operations. They gain hands-on experience in a controlled environment, improving their skills and confidence before performing procedures on actual patients.

8. Creative Workshops

Explanation: Creative workshops offer hands-on experiences in artistic and creative fields, allowing participants to practice and enhance their skills through direct creation and experimentation.

Example: In a painting workshop, participants learn various techniques and styles by actively creating their own artwork. The hands-on experience helps them develop technical skills, explore their creativity, and gain confidence in their artistic abilities.

Conclusion

Hands-on experiences such as coding bootcamps, business simulations, laboratory experiments, internships, design thinking workshops, community service projects, simulation-based training, and creative workshops illustrate the power of experiential learning. These examples show how applying knowledge in practical contexts not only reinforces learning but also builds valuable skills and insights. Embrace experiential learning opportunities to enhance your understanding, develop expertise, and achieve your educational and professional goals.

Chapter 4
Integrating Learning into Daily Life

Creating a Learning Routine

Practical Tips for Incorporating Learning into a Busy Schedule

Integrating learning into a busy schedule can be challenging but highly rewarding. By establishing a structured routine, you can ensure that learning becomes a consistent part of your daily life. Here are practical tips to help you create and maintain a learning routine amidst a busy schedule:

1. Set Clear Learning Goals

Explanation: Establishing specific, achievable goals helps you focus your learning efforts and measure progress.

Tips:
- ➢ **Define Objectives:** Determine what you want to achieve with your learning, such as mastering a new skill or gaining knowledge in a particular area.
- ➢ **Break Down Goals:** Divide larger goals into smaller, manageable tasks or milestones.

> **Set Deadlines:** Assign deadlines to each milestone to stay motivated and on track.

Example: If you want to learn a new language, set a goal to complete a certain number of lessons per week and achieve conversational fluency within six months.

2. Schedule Dedicated Learning Time

Explanation: Allocating specific times for learning ensures that it becomes a regular part of your routine.

Tips:

> **Choose Optimal Times:** Identify times when you are most alert and can focus, such as early mornings or evenings.

> **Use Time Blocks:** Dedicate blocks of time for learning, such as 30 minutes a day, and add these blocks to your calendar.

> **Consistency is Key:** Stick to your scheduled times consistently to build a learning habit.

Example: Set aside 30 minutes each morning before work to practice coding or read a chapter from a professional development book.

3. Incorporate Learning into Daily Activities

Explanation: Integrate learning into routine activities to make it easier to fit into your schedule.

Tips:

> **Listen to Educational Content:** Use commute time or exercise sessions to listen to podcasts or audiobooks related to your learning goals.

- **Use Waiting Time:** Utilize time spent waiting, such as during appointments or while waiting for the bus, to review notes or complete short learning activities.

- **Combine Learning with Other Tasks:** Engage in learning activities that complement your daily tasks, such as watching tutorials related to hobbies or professional interests.

Example: Listen to a business strategy podcast while driving to work or follow a language learning app during your daily workout.

4. Utilize Technology and Tools

Explanation: Leverage technology to streamline and enhance your learning process.

Tips:

- **Use Learning Apps:** Download apps that offer bite-sized lessons or quizzes to fit learning into short time periods.

- **Set Reminders:** Use calendar apps or task management tools to set reminders for your learning sessions.

- **Track Progress:** Use digital tools to track your progress and stay motivated.

Example: Use a language learning app like Duolingo that offers daily challenges and notifications to remind you to practice regularly.

5. Create a Learning-Friendly Environment

Explanation: Designate a space and resources that support your learning efforts.

Tips:

> ➤ **Set Up a Study Area:** Create a dedicated, clutter-free space for learning with all necessary materials and tools.
>
> ➤ **Minimize Distractions:** Ensure your learning environment is free from distractions to enhance focus and productivity.
>
> ➤ **Organize Resources:** Keep your learning materials, notes, and resources well-organized for easy access.

Example: Set up a corner of your home with a comfortable chair, desk, and all your study materials for focused learning sessions.

6. Balance Learning with Rest and Recreation

Explanation: Balancing learning with rest and leisure helps prevent burnout and maintains overall well-being.

Tips:

> ➤ **Schedule Breaks:** Incorporate regular breaks into your learning routine to rest and recharge.
>
> ➤ **Prioritize Self-Care:** Ensure you allocate time for relaxation, exercise, and hobbies to maintain a healthy balance.

> **Avoid Overloading:** Don't overload your schedule with too many learning tasks; allow flexibility for adjustments.

Example: After a focused learning session, take a short break to go for a walk or practice a hobby to refresh your mind and body.

7. Engage in Active Learning

Explanation: Active learning techniques, such as discussion and application, make learning more engaging and effective.

Tips:

> **Join Study Groups:** Participate in study groups or discussion forums to interact with others and share knowledge.

> **Apply What You Learn:** Use your newly acquired knowledge in real-world scenarios or projects to reinforce learning.

> **Teach Others:** Explaining concepts to others helps solidify your understanding and retention.

Example: Join an online forum related to your field of study to discuss topics and share insights with peers.

8. Reflect and Adjust

Explanation: Regular reflection and adjustment help optimize your learning routine and address any challenges.

Tips:

- ➢ **Reflect on Progress:** Periodically review your progress towards your learning goals and assess what's working and what's not.

- ➢ **Adjust as Needed:** Make adjustments to your routine based on your reflections, such as changing learning times or methods if needed.

- ➢ **Seek Feedback:** Get feedback from mentors or peers to identify areas for improvement.

Example: After a month of following your learning routine, assess your progress and adjust your schedule or methods based on your experiences and feedback.

Conclusion

Creating a learning routine involves setting clear goals, scheduling dedicated time, integrating learning into daily activities, using technology, creating a supportive environment, balancing with rest, engaging actively, and reflecting regularly. By implementing these practical tips, you can effectively incorporate learning into your busy schedule, achieve your educational goals, and continuously grow both personally and professionally. Embrace these strategies to make learning a seamless and rewarding part of your daily life.

Setting Realistic Learning Goals and Milestones

Setting realistic learning goals and milestones is essential for creating a structured and achievable learning routine. Clear goals and milestones provide direction, motivation, and a sense of progress. Here's how you can effectively set and manage your learning goals:

1. Define Clear and Specific Goals

Explanation: Clear and specific goals give you a concrete target to aim for, making it easier to measure progress and stay motivated.

Tips:

- ➢ **Be Specific:** Clearly articulate what you want to achieve. Avoid vague goals like "improve my writing" and instead set specific goals such as "write a 2,000-word essay on a given topic."

- ➢ **Use the SMART Framework:** Ensure your goals are Specific, Measurable, Achievable, Relevant, and Time-bound. This framework helps in creating goals that are both practical and motivating.

Example: Instead of "learn Spanish," set a specific goal like "complete Level 1 Spanish on the Duolingo app within three months."

2. Break Goals into Manageable Milestones

Explanation: Breaking larger goals into smaller, manageable milestones makes them less overwhelming and easier to track.

Tips:

- ➢ **Divide into Steps:** Identify the key steps or phases needed to achieve your main goal. This might include intermediate tasks or sub-goals.

> **Set Milestones:** Create milestones that represent significant achievements or progress points. These milestones act as checkpoints and keep you motivated.

Example: If your goal is to write a book, milestones might include outlining the chapters, writing a draft of each chapter, and editing the manuscript.

3. Prioritize Your Goals

Explanation: Prioritizing helps you focus on the most important or time-sensitive goals, ensuring that your efforts are aligned with your overall objectives.

Tips:

> **Assess Importance:** Determine which goals are most critical to your personal or professional growth and prioritize them.

> **Consider Timing:** Prioritize goals based on deadlines or urgency. For instance, a certification exam might take precedence over a long-term learning project.

Example: If you're aiming to improve your data analysis skills for an upcoming job promotion, prioritize this goal over other less time-sensitive learning activities.

4. Set Realistic Time Frames

Explanation: Realistic time frames ensure that your goals are achievable within the given period and help you maintain a manageable pace.

Tips:

- **Estimate Time Requirements:** Assess how long it will realistically take to achieve each milestone or goal based on your current skill level and available time.

- **Avoid Overambition:** Set time frames that are challenging but achievable, avoiding overly ambitious deadlines that could lead to frustration.

Example: Instead of aiming to complete a 10-week course in two weeks, set a more realistic timeframe of completing it in 10 weeks to ensure you absorb the material effectively.

5. Monitor and Adjust Goals

Explanation: Regularly monitoring and adjusting your goals ensures that they remain relevant and attainable as circumstances change.

Tips:

- **Track Progress:** Keep track of your progress towards each goal and milestone. Use tools like journals, apps, or spreadsheets to record achievements and setbacks.

- **Review and Adjust:** Periodically review your goals and milestones. Make adjustments based on your progress, changing priorities, or new insights.

Example: If you find that a particular study method isn't working well, adjust your approach or timeline to better suit your learning style and schedule.

6. Celebrate Achievements

Explanation: Celebrating milestones and achievements boosts motivation and reinforces your commitment to your learning goals.

Tips:

- **Acknowledge Success:** Take time to acknowledge and celebrate reaching milestones or completing goals. Recognize your hard work and achievements.

- **Reward Yourself:** Give yourself a reward or treat when you achieve a significant goal or milestone. This positive reinforcement helps maintain motivation.

Example: After completing a major project, reward yourself with a small celebration, such as a nice meal or a day off to relax.

7. Stay Flexible and Adaptable

Explanation: Flexibility allows you to adapt your goals and milestones based on changing circumstances or new opportunities.

Tips:

- **Embrace Changes:** Be open to adjusting your goals and milestones if needed. Life circumstances, new interests, or unexpected challenges might require modifications.

> **Adapt Strategies:** If your original plan isn't working as expected, adapt your strategies or approach to better fit your current situation.

Example: If an unexpected work project takes up more time than anticipated, adjust your learning goals or deadlines to accommodate the change without sacrificing progress.

8. Seek Feedback and Support

Explanation: Feedback and support from others can provide valuable insights and encouragement, helping you stay on track with your goals.

Tips:

> **Request Feedback:** Ask for feedback from mentors, peers, or colleagues on your progress and goals. Use their insights to make improvements.

> **Find Support:** Engage with a study group, mentor, or accountability partner to share your goals and progress. Their support can help keep you motivated.

Example: Share your learning goals with a mentor and request regular check-ins to discuss progress and receive guidance.

Conclusion

Setting realistic learning goals and milestones involves defining clear objectives, breaking them into manageable steps, prioritizing effectively, setting realistic time frames, monitoring progress, celebrating achievements, staying flexible, and seeking feedback. By implementing these strategies, you can create a structured and achievable learning routine that fits into your busy schedule and supports your personal and professional growth.

Finding Learning Opportunities in Everyday Life

Using Daily Experiences as Learning Opportunities

Learning doesn't always have to come from formal education or structured programs. Everyday experiences can offer valuable lessons and opportunities for growth. Here's how you can turn daily activities into learning opportunities:

1. Reflect on Daily Activities

Explanation: Regular reflection on your daily activities helps identify lessons and insights that you can apply to your personal and professional development.

Tips:

- ➤ **Keep a Journal:** Maintain a journal where you reflect on your daily experiences and note any insights or lessons learned.

- ➤ **Ask Questions:** After completing a task or activity, ask yourself what went well, what challenges you faced, and what you could improve.

> **Review Regularly:** Set aside time each week to review your reflections and identify patterns or recurring themes.

Example: After a team meeting, reflect on the effectiveness of your communication and consider how you can improve your presentation skills or address team dynamics.

2. Learn from Routine Tasks

Explanation: Routine tasks often provide opportunities to refine skills, discover efficiencies, and learn new approaches.

Tips:

> **Optimize Processes:** Look for ways to streamline or improve your routine tasks, such as finding more efficient methods or tools.

> **Experiment:** Try new techniques or tools in your routine tasks to see if they enhance productivity or outcomes.

> **Seek Feedback:** Ask for feedback from others involved in routine tasks to gain different perspectives and insights.

Example: If you're responsible for organizing team reports, experiment with different software tools to find one that improves your efficiency and accuracy.

3. Engage in Active Observation

Explanation: Observing people, environments, and situations actively can provide valuable learning experiences and insights.

Tips:

- ➤ **Observe Interactions:** Pay attention to how others handle challenges, communicate, or solve problems. Learn from their approaches and behaviors.

- ➤ **Analyze Environments:** Observe how different environments influence productivity or mood. Adapt your own environment based on these observations.

- ➤ **Note Innovations:** Keep an eye out for innovative solutions or practices in everyday settings and consider how they might apply to your own work or life.

Example: Observe how a colleague manages a difficult client interaction and consider applying their strategies to improve your own client communication skills.

4. Embrace Problem-Solving Situations

Explanation: Everyday problems and challenges offer opportunities to practice problem-solving skills and learn from the solutions you devise.

Tips:

- ➤ **Identify Problems:** Look for challenges or issues in your daily life that need addressing, whether at work or home.

- ➤ **Develop Solutions:** Work on finding solutions to these problems, and consider different approaches to solving them.

> **Evaluate Outcomes:** Assess the effectiveness of your solutions and learn from the outcomes, whether successful or not.

Example: If you encounter a recurring issue with time management, experiment with different scheduling techniques to find what works best for you.

5. Learn from Interactions with Others

Explanation: Interacting with people from various backgrounds and perspectives can offer valuable learning experiences and broaden your understanding.

Tips:

> **Engage in Conversations:** Initiate conversations with people who have different viewpoints or expertise. Learn from their experiences and insights.

> **Participate in Networking:** Attend networking events or social gatherings to meet new people and gain diverse perspectives.

> **Seek Mentorship:** Connect with mentors or advisors who can provide guidance and share their knowledge.

Example: Engage in conversations with colleagues from different departments to understand their roles and challenges, gaining insights that may inform your own work.

6. Apply Learning to Personal Interests

Explanation: Integrating learning into your personal interests and hobbies can make it more enjoyable and relevant.

Tips:

> ➤ **Incorporate Learning into Hobbies:** Use your hobbies as a platform for learning new skills or knowledge. For example, if you enjoy cooking, explore new recipes or culinary techniques.

> ➤ **Set Personal Challenges:** Challenge yourself to learn something new related to your personal interests, such as mastering a musical instrument or improving your gardening skills.

> ➤ **Share with Others:** Share your learning experiences and discoveries with friends or family to reinforce your knowledge and gain new perspectives.

Example: If you love photography, experiment with advanced techniques and editing software to enhance your skills and capture better images.

7. Turn Mistakes into Learning Opportunities

Explanation: Mistakes and setbacks provide valuable lessons and opportunities for growth if approached with a learning mindset.

Tips:

> ➤ **Analyze Mistakes:** Reflect on what went wrong and identify the underlying causes. Use this analysis to learn and improve.

> **Adopt a Growth Mindset:** Embrace mistakes as learning opportunities rather than failures. Focus on what you can learn and how you can apply it moving forward.

> **Make Adjustments:** Implement changes based on what you've learned from mistakes to prevent similar issues in the future.

Example: If a project fails to meet expectations, analyze what led to the shortcomings and adjust your approach or processes for future projects.

8. Leverage Everyday Technology

Explanation: Everyday technology, such as apps and online resources, can offer continuous learning opportunities.

Tips:

> **Use Learning Apps:** Explore apps and platforms that offer educational content or skill-building exercises related to your interests.

> **Follow Educational Content:** Subscribe to blogs, newsletters, or social media accounts that provide valuable information and updates in your field.

> **Set Learning Alerts:** Use technology to set reminders or notifications for educational content or learning activities.

Example: Use a language learning app to practice a new language during your daily commute or follow an industry blog to stay updated on trends and developments.

Conclusion

Finding learning opportunities in everyday life involves reflecting on daily activities, learning from routine tasks, engaging in active observation, embracing problem-solving situations, learning from interactions with others, applying learning to personal interests, turning mistakes into lessons, and leveraging everyday technology. By integrating these practices into your routine, you can make continuous learning a natural and enriching part of your daily life, enhancing both personal and professional growth.

Incorporating Learning into Hobbies, Travel, and Social Interactions

Learning can be seamlessly woven into various aspects of your life, including hobbies, travel, and social interactions. By integrating learning into these areas, you can enhance your experiences and continuously grow without requiring additional time commitments. Here's how to incorporate learning into these aspects of your life:

1. Learning Through Hobbies

Explanation: Hobbies provide a natural and enjoyable context for learning new skills and knowledge. Engaging in hobbies can enhance your expertise and offer personal satisfaction.

Tips:

- **Expand Skills:** Use your hobby as a platform to explore new techniques or deepen your knowledge. For example, if you enjoy painting, experiment with different styles or mediums.

- **Join Clubs or Groups:** Participate in hobby-related clubs or online communities to learn from others and share experiences.

- **Set Learning Goals:** Challenge yourself with specific learning objectives related to your hobby. This could involve mastering a particular technique or creating a series of projects.

Example: If you're passionate about gardening, learn about advanced techniques such as hydroponics or organic farming. Join a local gardening club to exchange tips and experiences with fellow enthusiasts.

2. Learning Through Travel

Explanation: Traveling exposes you to new cultures, languages, and experiences, providing ample learning opportunities. Embrace these experiences to gain a broader perspective and enrich your knowledge.

Tips:

- **Research Destinations:** Before traveling, research the history, culture, and local customs of your destination. This preparation enhances your experience and understanding.

- **Engage Locally:** Interact with locals, participate in cultural events, and explore local traditions to gain firsthand knowledge about different cultures.

> **Reflect and Document:** After your trip, reflect on your experiences and document what you've learned. Share your insights with others or use them to enhance your personal or professional projects.

Example: During a trip to Japan, learn basic Japanese phrases, visit historical sites, and try traditional cuisine. Document your experiences and share them through a blog or social media.

3. Learning Through Social Interactions

Explanation: Social interactions provide opportunities to learn from others, gain new perspectives, and enhance your communication and interpersonal skills.

Tips:

> **Ask Questions:** Engage in conversations with people from diverse backgrounds and ask questions to learn about their experiences, opinions, and expertise.

> **Attend Events:** Participate in social events, networking gatherings, or community activities to meet new people and learn from their experiences.

> **Share Knowledge:** Teach others what you know, as explaining concepts helps reinforce your understanding and opens up opportunities for learning from their feedback.

Example: Attend industry conferences or local meetups to connect with professionals and gain insights into emerging trends and best practices. Share your own knowledge and experiences to foster meaningful discussions.

4. Combining Learning with Everyday Activities

Explanation: Integrate learning into routine activities to make it a seamless part of your day-to-day life.

Tips:

> - **Listen to Educational Content:** Use commute time or other idle moments to listen to audiobooks, podcasts, or lectures related to your interests or goals.
>
> - **Incorporate Learning into Chores:** Turn routine chores into learning opportunities by listening to educational content or practicing new skills while you work.
>
> - **Set Learning Challenges:** Challenge yourself to learn something new each day or week, incorporating it into your daily activities.

Example: While cooking dinner, listen to a podcast about culinary techniques or a book on nutrition to enhance your cooking skills and knowledge.

5. Learning Through Volunteering and Community Involvement

Explanation: Volunteering and community involvement provide opportunities to learn new skills, gain diverse experiences, and contribute to meaningful causes.

Tips:

- **Volunteer for New Roles:** Take on different roles or responsibilities within volunteer organizations to learn new skills and gain varied experiences.

- **Participate in Community Projects:** Engage in community projects or initiatives to learn about different social issues and contribute to positive change.

- **Network and Collaborate:** Connect with other volunteers and community members to share knowledge and learn from their experiences.

Example: Volunteer at a local non-profit organization to gain experience in project management or event planning. Collaborate with others to learn about different perspectives and approaches.

6. Continuous Reflection and Adaptation

Explanation: Regular reflection on your learning experiences helps you identify what's working and make adjustments to enhance your growth.

Tips:

- **Reflect on Experiences:** After engaging in hobbies, travel, or social interactions, take time to reflect on what you've learned and how it has impacted you.

- **Adapt and Evolve:** Use your reflections to adapt your learning strategies or incorporate new approaches based on your experiences.

> **Document Insights:** Keep a journal or record of your learning experiences to track progress and identify areas for further exploration.

Example: After participating in a community event, reflect on the skills you've gained and consider how you can apply them to other areas of your life or future projects.

Conclusion

Incorporating learning into hobbies, travel, and social interactions involves leveraging these experiences to enhance your knowledge and personal growth. By expanding skills through hobbies, embracing cultural insights during travel, learning from social interactions, integrating learning into everyday activities, and engaging in volunteering, you can make learning a natural and enriching part of your life. Embrace these opportunities to continuously grow and develop, turning everyday experiences into valuable learning moments.

Chapter 5
Overcoming Learning Challenges

Common Obstacles

Identifying and Addressing Barriers to Lifelong Learning

Lifelong learning is a valuable and ongoing process, but it's not without its challenges. Identifying and overcoming common obstacles can help you stay committed to your learning journey. Here's how to address some of the most frequent barriers:

1. Lack of Time

Explanation: Finding time for learning amid busy schedules can be a significant challenge. However, with effective time management, you can integrate learning into your daily life.

Tips:

- **Prioritize Learning:** Schedule dedicated time for learning just as you would for other important activities. Even short, regular sessions can be effective.

- **Use Micro-Learning:** Break learning into small, manageable chunks that fit into your available time. For example, spend 10-15 minutes each day on a language learning app.

➢ **Combine Learning with Daily Activities:** Utilize downtime, such as commuting or waiting, to engage in learning activities like listening to educational podcasts or audiobooks.

Example: If your schedule is packed, allocate 20 minutes each morning to read an educational article or watch a tutorial video. Integrate learning into your routine tasks, like listening to a podcast during your commute.

2. Lack of Motivation

Explanation: Staying motivated can be difficult, especially when progress seems slow or when facing obstacles. Finding ways to maintain motivation is crucial for sustained learning.

Tips:

➢ **Set Clear Goals:** Define specific, achievable learning goals and milestones to create a sense of purpose and direction.

➢ **Find Personal Relevance:** Connect learning to your personal interests, career goals, or life aspirations to make it more engaging and meaningful.

➢ **Celebrate Progress:** Acknowledge and celebrate your achievements, no matter how small. Recognizing progress helps maintain motivation and encourages continued effort.

Example: If you're struggling with motivation to learn a new skill, relate it to a personal goal, such as using the skill to start a side project or advance in your career. Reward yourself for reaching milestones.

3. Overwhelm from Too Much Information

Explanation: The vast amount of information available can be overwhelming and make it challenging to focus on what's most relevant for your learning goals.

Tips:

- **Filter Information:** Identify reliable sources and focus on quality over quantity. Choose resources that are directly aligned with your learning objectives.

- **Create a Learning Plan:** Develop a structured plan that outlines what you need to learn, the resources to use, and the timeline for achieving your goals.

- **Avoid Perfectionism:** Recognize that you don't need to learn everything at once. Prioritize key areas and tackle them gradually.

Example: If you're learning a new subject, start with foundational resources and gradually build up your knowledge. Avoid getting bogged down by every detail or resource available.

4. Lack of Support

Explanation: Without support from others, it can be challenging to stay accountable and motivated in your learning efforts.

Tips:

➢ **Seek Mentorship:** Find a mentor or advisor who can provide guidance, feedback, and encouragement throughout your learning journey.

➢ **Join Learning Communities:** Participate in study groups, online forums, or local learning communities to connect with others who share similar interests and goals.

➢ **Share Your Goals:** Communicate your learning objectives with friends, family, or colleagues to gain their support and accountability.

Example: Join an online course or local workshop where you can interact with peers and instructors. Share your learning goals with a friend or colleague who can help keep you accountable.

5. Financial Constraints

Explanation: The cost of educational resources, courses, or certifications can be a barrier to accessing learning opportunities.

Tips:

➢ **Utilize Free Resources:** Take advantage of free or low-cost learning resources available online, such as MOOCs (Massive Open Online Courses), webinars, and educational videos.

➢ **Apply for Scholarships or Grants:** Look for scholarships, grants, or financial aid options that can help cover the cost of formal education or training programs.

> **Invest Wisely:** Prioritize investments in learning that offer the greatest return on investment in terms of personal or professional growth.

Example: Use platforms like Coursera, edX, or Khan Academy for free courses and resources. Apply for scholarships or financial aid for more advanced certifications or degrees.

6. Balancing Learning with Other Responsibilities

Explanation: Balancing learning with work, family, and other responsibilities can be challenging, especially when trying to fit learning into an already busy life.

Tips:

> **Integrate Learning into Existing Routines:** Find ways to incorporate learning into your daily routines, such as listening to educational content while doing household chores.

> **Manage Time Effectively:** Use time management techniques to allocate dedicated periods for learning, while still fulfilling other responsibilities.

> **Set Realistic Expectations:** Adjust your learning goals and expectations based on your available time and other commitments. Recognize that progress may be gradual.

Example: If you have a demanding job and family responsibilities, set aside a specific time each week for focused learning. Adjust your goals to match the time you can realistically commit.

7. Fear of Failure or Lack of Confidence

Explanation: Fear of failure or lack of confidence can hinder your willingness to start or continue learning new skills.

Tips:

> - **Adopt a Growth Mindset:** Embrace the idea that learning involves experimentation and occasional setbacks. View challenges as opportunities to grow rather than as failures.
> - **Start Small:** Begin with small, manageable learning tasks to build confidence and gradually tackle more complex challenges.
> - **Seek Encouragement:** Surround yourself with supportive people who can provide encouragement and reassurance.

Example: If you're hesitant to start a new learning project due to fear of failure, begin with a small project or skill. Celebrate your progress and use it as motivation to tackle more challenging tasks.

8. Limited Access to Resources

Explanation: Access to educational resources can be limited due to geographic location, technology constraints, or other factors.

Tips:

- **Leverage Online Resources:** Use online platforms and digital libraries to access a wide range of educational materials and courses.

- **Explore Community Resources:** Look for local libraries, community centers, or educational institutions that offer free or low-cost resources and programs.

- **Connect with Others:** Network with individuals or groups who may have access to resources or knowledge that can benefit your learning.

Example: If you lack access to formal education resources, utilize online platforms like YouTube for tutorials or connect with online communities for shared resources and knowledge.

Conclusion

Overcoming common obstacles to lifelong learning involves identifying challenges such as lack of time, motivation, overwhelm, support, financial constraints, balancing responsibilities, fear of failure, and limited access to resources. By implementing strategies like prioritizing learning, seeking support, setting realistic goals, and utilizing available resources, you can address these barriers and maintain a continuous and enriching learning journey. Embrace these solutions to stay committed to your personal and professional growth despite the challenges you may encounter.

Strategies for Staying Motivated

Techniques for Maintaining Enthusiasm and Commitment to Learning

Maintaining motivation and enthusiasm for learning can be challenging, especially over the long term. Here are several effective strategies to help you stay committed and keep your learning journey engaging:

1. Set Clear, Achievable Goals

Explanation: Having well-defined goals provides direction and purpose, making it easier to stay motivated. Break down larger goals into smaller, manageable milestones to create a sense of accomplishment along the way.

Tips:

- **Define Specific Goals:** Clearly articulate what you want to achieve with your learning, such as mastering a new skill or earning a certification.

- **Create Milestones:** Set intermediate goals or milestones that you can celebrate as you progress. These smaller achievements help maintain motivation.

- **Track Progress:** Use a journal, app, or planner to track your progress towards your goals and milestones.

Example: If your goal is to learn a new programming language, set specific milestones like completing a beginner's course, building a small project, and contributing to an open-source project.

2. Connect Learning to Personal Interests

Explanation: When learning aligns with your personal interests or passions, it becomes more enjoyable and engaging. Connecting new knowledge to what excites you can enhance motivation.

Tips:

- **Choose Relevant Topics:** Select learning topics that are directly related to your interests or hobbies. This makes the learning process more enjoyable.
- **Apply Learning to Interests:** Use what you learn to enhance your hobbies or personal projects. For example, apply new skills in photography to create unique art pieces.
- **Stay Curious:** Explore how your learning can connect with broader interests or future aspirations.

Example: If you're passionate about cooking, learn new culinary techniques and apply them to experiment with innovative recipes or host cooking classes.

3. Create a Learning Routine

Explanation: Establishing a regular learning routine helps make learning a consistent part of your daily or weekly schedule. Consistency builds habits and keeps you on track.

Tips:

- ➤ **Schedule Learning Time:** Set aside specific times each day or week dedicated to learning. Treat it as a non-negotiable appointment.

- ➤ **Develop a Routine:** Create a structured routine that includes a mix of different learning activities to keep things fresh and engaging.

- ➤ **Stick to the Plan:** Adhere to your routine as closely as possible to build discipline and maintain momentum.

Example: Allocate 30 minutes each morning to study a new language, and another 30 minutes in the evening to work on a related project or practice speaking.

4. Use Positive Reinforcement

Explanation: Rewarding yourself for achieving learning milestones or completing tasks can reinforce positive behavior and keep you motivated.

Tips:

- ➤ **Set Rewards:** Determine rewards for reaching specific goals or milestones, such as enjoying a favorite treat, taking a day off, or buying something you've been wanting.

- ➤ **Celebrate Achievements:** Take time to celebrate your progress and achievements, no matter how small. Acknowledging success boosts morale and motivation.

> **Share Success:** Share your accomplishments with friends, family, or a community to receive positive feedback and encouragement.

Example: Reward yourself with a movie night or a special outing after completing a challenging module or finishing a major project.

5. Stay Accountable

Explanation: Accountability helps keep you on track by creating a sense of responsibility and commitment. Having someone to report to or share progress with can enhance motivation.

Tips:

> **Find an Accountability Partner:** Partner with a friend, mentor, or colleague who can support your learning goals and check in on your progress.

> **Join a Study Group:** Participate in study groups or learning communities where members share their goals and progress, providing mutual support and accountability.

> **Set Regular Check-Ins:** Schedule regular check-ins with your accountability partner or group to discuss progress, challenges, and strategies for overcoming obstacles.

Example: Join a learning group or find a study buddy who shares your goals. Schedule weekly meetings to discuss progress, challenges, and strategies.

6. Maintain a Growth Mindset

Explanation: Embracing a growth mindset—believing that abilities and intelligence can be developed through effort and learning—helps you stay motivated and resilient.

Tips:

- **Focus on Effort, Not Just Results:** Celebrate the effort and progress made, rather than solely focusing on outcomes. Recognize that setbacks are part of the learning process.

- **Embrace Challenges:** View challenges as opportunities to grow and improve. Approach difficulties with a positive attitude and a willingness to learn from them.

- **Reflect on Growth:** Regularly reflect on your growth and development. Acknowledge how far you've come and how your learning has contributed to your personal and professional growth.

Example: If you encounter a difficult concept, approach it with curiosity and determination. Reflect on how overcoming this challenge contributes to your overall growth and learning journey.

7. Incorporate Variety in Learning

Explanation: Introducing variety into your learning activities keeps things interesting and prevents boredom. Mixing up your methods and resources can enhance engagement and motivation.

Tips:

- **Explore Different Formats:** Use a variety of learning formats, such as videos, books, podcasts, and interactive tools, to keep your learning experience diverse.

- **Try New Approaches:** Experiment with different learning methods, such as hands-on projects, group discussions, or practical applications.

- **Stay Curious:** Continuously seek out new topics or areas of interest to keep your learning experience dynamic and stimulating.

Example: If you're learning about digital marketing, explore online courses, read industry blogs, listen to relevant podcasts, and apply what you learn through hands-on projects.

8. Visualize Success

Explanation: Visualization helps reinforce your commitment and motivation by creating a clear mental picture of your goals and the rewards of achieving them.

Tips:

- **Create Vision Boards:** Develop a vision board with images, quotes, and goals that represent your learning objectives and aspirations.

- **Practice Visualization:** Spend a few minutes each day visualizing your success and the positive impact it will have on your life or career.

> **Stay Focused on Outcomes:** Regularly remind yourself of the benefits and rewards of achieving your learning goals to maintain motivation.

Example: Create a vision board with images representing your learning goals, such as a new job title or skill certification. Use it to remind yourself of the rewards and benefits of your efforts.

Conclusion

Staying motivated for lifelong learning involves setting clear goals, connecting learning to personal interests, creating a routine, using positive reinforcement, maintaining accountability, embracing a growth mindset, incorporating variety, and visualizing success. By implementing these strategies, you can overcome challenges, keep your enthusiasm high, and maintain a consistent commitment to your learning journey. Embrace these techniques to stay engaged and inspired as you pursue continuous growth and development.

Dealing with Setbacks:

How to Overcome Setbacks and Stay on Track with Learning Goals

Setbacks are an inevitable part of any learning journey. Whether it's a missed deadline, a challenging concept, or unexpected life events, knowing how to effectively deal with setbacks can help you stay on track and continue progressing towards your learning goals. Here are strategies for overcoming setbacks and maintaining your momentum:

1. Accept and Acknowledge Setbacks

Explanation: The first step in overcoming setbacks is to acknowledge and accept them. Recognize that setbacks are a natural part of the learning process and that they don't define your abilities or potential.

Tips:

- **Stay Positive:** Maintain a positive attitude and remind yourself that setbacks are opportunities to learn and grow.

- **Reflect on the Setback:** Take time to understand what caused the setback and how it affects your learning progress.

- **Avoid Self-Criticism:** Refrain from being overly critical of yourself. Instead, focus on solutions and how to move forward.

Example: If you miss a deadline for a project, acknowledge the setback without dwelling on it. Reflect on what led to the delay and how you can adjust your approach to prevent similar issues in the future.

2. Analyze the Cause and Adjust Your Plan

Explanation: Identifying the root cause of a setback can help you make necessary adjustments to your learning plan. Understanding why a setback occurred allows you to address any underlying issues and improve your approach.

Tips:

- **Identify Contributing Factors:** Determine the factors that contributed to the setback, such as lack of preparation, external interruptions, or unrealistic goals.

- ➤ **Adjust Your Strategies:** Modify your learning plan or strategies based on the insights gained. This may involve changing your study habits, revising goals, or seeking additional resources.

- ➤ **Set New Milestones:** Create new milestones or deadlines that accommodate any changes to your plan, ensuring they are realistic and achievable.

Example: If you struggled with a particular topic in a course, analyze whether the issue was due to a lack of understanding, insufficient practice, or time management. Adjust your study plan to address these factors.

3. Develop a Resilience Mindset

Explanation: Building resilience helps you bounce back from setbacks and continue moving forward. Cultivating a resilient mindset enables you to face challenges with determination and perseverance.

Tips:

- ➤ **Embrace Challenges:** View setbacks as challenges to overcome rather than obstacles to success. Embrace them as part of your learning journey.

- ➤ **Stay Focused on the Long-Term Goal:** Keep your long-term learning goals in mind and remind yourself of the bigger picture.

> **Practice Self-Care:** Take care of your physical and emotional well-being to maintain resilience. Engage in activities that reduce stress and promote mental health.

Example: If you encounter a significant obstacle, such as failing an exam, use it as an opportunity to strengthen your resilience. Focus on how you can use this experience to enhance your future learning efforts.

4. Seek Support and Guidance

Explanation: Seeking support from mentors, peers, or professionals can provide valuable insights and encouragement when dealing with setbacks. Having a support network can help you stay motivated and find solutions to challenges.

Tips:

> **Reach Out to Mentors:** Consult with mentors or advisors who can provide guidance and advice on overcoming setbacks.

> **Join Support Groups:** Participate in study groups or online communities where you can share experiences and receive support from others facing similar challenges.

> **Seek Professional Help:** If setbacks are significantly impacting your progress, consider seeking professional help, such as a career counselor or coach.

Example: If you're struggling with a specific skill, reach out to a mentor or join a study group where you can get feedback and support from others.

5. Reevaluate and Revise Goals

Explanation: Sometimes setbacks indicate that your goals or plans may need to be revised. Reassessing your goals ensures they remain relevant and achievable, helping you stay focused and motivated.

Tips:

> ➢ **Review Your Goals:** Periodically review your learning goals to ensure they align with your current needs and circumstances.
>
> ➢ **Adjust Expectations:** Set realistic and flexible goals that accommodate potential setbacks and changes in your learning journey.
>
> ➢ **Break Down Goals:** Divide larger goals into smaller, manageable tasks to make progress more achievable and less overwhelming.

Example: If you find that a long-term goal is no longer feasible due to recent setbacks, revise your goals to reflect a more attainable timeframe and adjust your plan accordingly.

6. Learn from the Setback

Explanation: Every setback provides an opportunity for learning and growth. Reflect on what you can learn from the experience to improve your future efforts and approach.

Tips:

- **Analyze the Experience:** Reflect on the setback and identify lessons learned or insights gained that can help you avoid similar issues in the future.

- **Adjust Your Approach:** Use the knowledge gained to make improvements to your learning strategies or methods.

- **Implement Changes:** Apply the lessons learned to your ongoing learning efforts to enhance your resilience and effectiveness.

Example: If you encountered a challenge with time management, use the experience to implement new strategies for balancing your learning schedule with other responsibilities.

7. Maintain Flexibility and Adaptability

Explanation: Flexibility and adaptability are key to managing setbacks effectively. Being open to adjusting your plans and approaches can help you navigate challenges and stay on track.

Tips:

- **Be Open to Change:** Embrace changes to your learning plan or goals as necessary. Adaptability helps you respond effectively to unexpected challenges.

- **Experiment with New Strategies:** Try different learning methods or approaches if your current ones aren't working as expected.

> **Stay Positive:** Maintain a positive outlook and remain adaptable in the face of setbacks.

Example: If a particular learning method isn't yielding the desired results, be open to experimenting with alternative approaches or tools to achieve your goals.

8. Celebrate Resilience and Progress

Explanation: Acknowledging and celebrating your ability to overcome setbacks reinforces a positive mindset and motivates you to continue pursuing your goals.

Tips:

> **Recognize Efforts:** Take time to appreciate the effort and resilience demonstrated in overcoming setbacks.

> **Celebrate Successes:** Reward yourself for successfully navigating challenges and reaching milestones, no matter how small.

> **Reflect on Achievements:** Regularly reflect on your progress and achievements to maintain a sense of accomplishment.

Example: After overcoming a significant setback, celebrate your resilience by treating yourself to a special activity or reflecting on the progress you've made.

Conclusion

Dealing with setbacks involves accepting and acknowledging challenges, analyzing causes, developing resilience, seeking support, revising goals, learning from experiences, maintaining flexibility, and celebrating progress. By implementing these strategies, you can effectively manage setbacks, stay on track with your learning goals, and continue progressing towards your aspirations. Embrace setbacks as opportunities for growth and use them to strengthen your commitment to lifelong learning.

Chapter 6
Inspiring Stories of Transformation

Success Stories

Profiles of Individuals Who Have Achieved Significant Personal Growth Through Lifelong Learning

Lifelong learning has the power to transform lives, helping individuals achieve their dreams, overcome challenges, and realize their full potential. In this chapter, we will explore the inspiring stories of individuals who have embraced lifelong learning and experienced remarkable personal growth. These stories demonstrate how continuous learning can lead to significant achievements and enrich one's life.

1. The Journey of Sarah: From Career Change to Entrepreneurial Success

Background: Sarah was a mid-level manager in a corporate job who felt unfulfilled and wanted to make a significant career change. At 35, she decided to pursue her passion for baking and started taking evening classes in pastry arts while still working full-time.

Transformation: Sarah's dedication to learning and her passion for baking led her to acquire advanced skills and knowledge in culinary arts. She began experimenting with new recipes, participated in baking competitions, and built a strong network within the food industry. After three years of balancing her job and studies, she launched her own bakery.

Outcome: Today, Sarah runs a successful bakery with multiple locations. Her commitment to lifelong learning allowed her to turn her passion into a thriving business. Sarah's story highlights how pursuing learning opportunities can lead to a rewarding career transformation and personal fulfillment.

2. David's Quest: From Engineer to Author and Public Speaker

Background: David, an engineer with over a decade of experience in the tech industry, always had a keen interest in writing and public speaking. Despite a demanding job, he took online courses in creative writing and public speaking during his weekends.

Transformation: David's learning journey empowered him to write and publish his first book on technology and innovation. He also started giving talks at industry conferences and workshops, sharing his insights and expertise with others. His efforts paid off as he gained recognition as an influential author and sought-after speaker.

Outcome: David's dedication to continuous learning opened new career paths and opportunities, enabling him to transition from engineering to becoming a successful author and public speaker. His story illustrates how embracing lifelong learning can expand professional horizons and create new avenues for success.

3. Maria's Reinvention: From Teacher to Global Education Advocate

Background: Maria, a retired schoolteacher in her early 60s, was looking for new ways to stay engaged and make a difference after retirement. She decided to take online courses in educational technology and global education.

Transformation: Maria's new skills and knowledge led her to become a global education advocate. She volunteered with international organizations, developed educational resources, and spoke at global conferences about innovative teaching methods. Her work had a significant impact on education in underserved communities.

Outcome: Maria's commitment to lifelong learning allowed her to reinvent herself and contribute meaningfully to global education. Her story exemplifies how learning new skills in later life can lead to impactful and fulfilling new roles.

4. Amit's Resilience: From Unemployment to Tech Innovator

Background: Amit, a recent college graduate, faced unemployment for several months despite his engineering degree. Determined to improve his prospects, he enrolled in online courses on data science and machine learning.

Transformation: Amit's proactive approach to learning enabled him to acquire in-demand skills in a rapidly growing field. He worked on personal projects, contributed to open-source initiatives, and eventually secured a position at a leading tech company. His skills and expertise led him to innovate new solutions for data analysis and artificial intelligence.

Outcome: Amit's story demonstrates how lifelong learning can turn challenging situations into opportunities for career advancement and innovation. His resilience and commitment to acquiring new skills led to significant personal and professional growth.

5. Jessica's Journey: From Corporate Lawyer to Non-Profit Leader

Background: Jessica, a successful corporate lawyer, felt a growing desire to contribute to social causes. She decided to pursue courses in non-profit management and social entrepreneurship while continuing her legal career.

Transformation: With her newfound knowledge and passion, Jessica transitioned into the non-profit sector. She founded a non-profit organization dedicated to improving access to education for underprivileged children. Her legal expertise and learning in non-profit management helped her build a successful and impactful organization.

Outcome: Jessica's commitment to lifelong learning enabled her to pivot from a lucrative legal career to making a meaningful difference in the non-profit sector.

Her story highlights how learning and pursuing passions can lead to impactful and fulfilling career changes.

6. Liam's Digital Transition: From Traditional Artist to Digital Creator

Background: Liam was a traditional painter in his 50s who had always worked with physical media. As digital art began gaining popularity, he realized the need to adapt to new technology.

Transformation: Liam enrolled in online courses to learn digital art techniques and software. His commitment to mastering digital tools allowed him to create stunning digital artworks and reach a broader audience through social media and online galleries.

Outcome: Liam's transition to digital art not only rejuvenated his career but also opened up new opportunities for exhibitions and collaborations. His story illustrates how embracing digital skills can refresh and expand artistic careers.

7. Nina's Academic Pursuit: From High School Teacher to Research Scholar

Background: Nina, a high school biology teacher in her late 40s, was passionate about advancing her knowledge in her field. She felt the need to delve deeper into scientific research.

Transformation: Nina pursued a part-time master's degree and eventually a Ph.D. in biological sciences. She engaged in research projects and published papers in scientific journals.

Outcome: Nina's commitment to lifelong learning led to a significant shift in her career from teaching to conducting advanced research. Her story highlights how academic advancement can lead to new professional opportunities and contributions to one's field.

8. Raj's Tech Upgrade: From Manual Worker to IT Specialist

Background: Raj, a manual laborer in his early 40s, wanted to enhance his career prospects and adapt to the growing tech industry.

Transformation: Raj took advantage of online coding bootcamps and technical courses to gain skills in IT and software development. His dedication allowed him to transition into an IT support role and eventually specialize in cybersecurity.

Outcome: Raj's journey from manual labor to IT specialist demonstrates how acquiring new technical skills can lead to career advancement and open doors to emerging fields in technology.

9. Sophie's Lifelong Passion: From Stay-at-Home Mom to Published Author

Background: Sophie had been a stay-at-home mom for over a decade, dedicating her time to raising her children. Her passion for writing remained unfulfilled.

Transformation: Sophie enrolled in writing workshops and online courses to hone her craft. She wrote and self-published her first novel and built an online presence as an author.

Outcome: Sophie's commitment to pursuing her passion for writing led to the successful publication of her book and a new career as an author. Her story underscores the potential for lifelong learning to help individuals achieve personal dreams and new professional identities.

10. Amina's Technological Advancement: From Financial Analyst to Data Scientist

Background: Amina, a financial analyst in her early 30s, wanted to stay ahead in the rapidly evolving field of data analysis.

Transformation: Amina pursued advanced courses in data science and machine learning. She applied her new skills to solve complex problems in her field and gained certification as a data scientist.

Outcome: Amina's upskilling led to a promotion and recognition as a data scientist. Her story highlights how staying updated with industry trends and acquiring new skills can lead to career advancement and new opportunities.

11. Oscar's Retirement Reimagined: From Engineer to Community Educator

Background: Oscar, a retired engineer in his 60s, wanted to continue contributing to society and stay mentally active after retiring.

Transformation: Oscar took courses in community education and started volunteering to teach STEM subjects to local high school students. He developed engaging educational programs and workshops.

Outcome: Oscar's involvement in community education allowed him to share his expertise and make a positive impact on students' lives. His story reflects how lifelong learning can lead to fulfilling retirement activities and community contributions.

12. Elena's Entrepreneurial Spirit: From Corporate Executive to Startup Founder

Background: Elena, a corporate executive in her 40s, had always dreamed of starting her own business. She realized that she needed to learn about entrepreneurship and business management.

Transformation: Elena completed courses on entrepreneurship and startup management. She used her corporate experience and new knowledge to launch a successful tech startup.

Outcome: Elena's entrepreneurial venture flourished, demonstrating how lifelong learning can turn long-held dreams into reality and lead to successful business endeavors.

Conclusion

These diverse success stories highlight the transformative power of lifelong learning across different professions, ages, and backgrounds. Whether transitioning careers, pursuing passions, or enhancing skills, individuals who embrace continuous learning experience significant personal and professional growth. These stories serve as a testament to the endless possibilities that lifelong learning offers, encouraging readers to embark on their own journeys of transformation.

Lessons Learned

Key Takeaways and Common Themes from the Stories

The stories shared in this chapter reflect the diverse paths individuals have taken to achieve remarkable personal and professional growth through lifelong learning. Here are the key takeaways and common themes that can inspire and guide readers in their own learning journeys:

1. Embrace Continuous Learning as a Path to Change

Takeaway: Lifelong learning is not a one-time event but a continuous journey. Whether you're changing careers, pursuing new passions, or enhancing existing skills, embracing learning as a lifelong commitment opens doors to new opportunities and personal growth.

Example: Jessica's transition from a corporate lawyer to a non-profit leader exemplifies how continuous learning can lead to profound career shifts and meaningful impact.

2. Leverage New Skills to Innovate and Adapt

Takeaway: Acquiring new skills can help you adapt to changing industries and technological advancements. Staying current with emerging trends and technologies is essential for innovation and staying relevant in your field.

Example: Liam's shift from traditional art to digital art demonstrates how learning new techniques can refresh and expand your career.

3. Pursue Passion Projects to Fulfill Personal Goals

Takeaway: Lifelong learning can help you pursue long-held passions and personal dreams, leading to a more fulfilling and enriched life. By investing in what you love, you can turn hobbies into successful ventures.

Example: Sophie's journey from stay-at-home mom to published author highlights how pursuing personal interests through learning can lead to achieving significant life goals.

4. Adapt Learning to Different Life Stages

Takeaway: Lifelong learning is relevant at every stage of life. Whether you're transitioning to retirement, seeking new career paths, or enhancing your expertise, adapting learning strategies to your current stage can lead to new opportunities and growth.

Example: Oscar's transition from engineering to community education after retirement showcases how lifelong learning can create fulfilling post-retirement activities and contributions.

5. Integrate Learning with Professional Development

Takeaway: For professionals, continuous learning is crucial for career advancement and staying competitive. By integrating learning into your professional development strategy, you can enhance your skills and open new career pathways.

Example: Amina's shift from financial analyst to data scientist illustrates how continuous learning can lead to career advancement and new opportunities in a rapidly evolving field.

6. Leverage Learning Resources Effectively

Takeaway: Using a variety of learning resources, such as online courses, books, and practical experiences, can enhance your learning journey. Selecting high-quality resources and applying what you learn can significantly impact your growth.

Example: Raj's successful transition to IT specialist through online courses and self-study emphasizes the importance of utilizing effective learning resources to achieve career goals.

7. Stay Resilient and Adapt to Setbacks

Takeaway: Lifelong learning involves overcoming challenges and setbacks. Maintaining resilience and adapting to obstacles can help you stay on track and continue progressing toward your goals.

Example: David's journey from engineer to author and public speaker shows how resilience and adaptability in learning can lead to achieving new professional heights.

8. Find Learning Opportunities in Everyday Life

Takeaway: Learning doesn't have to be confined to formal settings. Everyday experiences, hobbies, travel, and social interactions can provide valuable learning opportunities that contribute to personal and professional development.

Example: Maria's use of her retirement to engage in global education advocacy highlights how integrating learning into daily life can lead to impactful contributions and personal satisfaction.

Conclusion

The key takeaways from these inspiring stories underscore the transformative power of lifelong learning. By embracing continuous learning, adapting to new skills, pursuing passions, and integrating learning into various aspects of life, individuals can achieve remarkable personal and professional growth. These lessons serve as a guide for readers to embark on their own learning journeys, demonstrating that with dedication and perseverance, lifelong learning can lead to extraordinary transformations and fulfilling achievements.

How Readers Can Apply These Lessons to Their Own Lives

The inspiring stories of individuals who have embraced lifelong learning demonstrate that personal and professional growth is within reach for anyone willing to invest in their own development. Here's how you, as a reader, can apply these lessons to your own life:

1. Adopt a Mindset of Continuous Learning

Application: Embrace the idea that learning is a lifelong process, not limited by age or stage of life. Commit to ongoing education and skill development, whether through formal education, online courses, or self-directed study.

Action Steps:
- Identify areas of interest or skills you want to develop.
- Create a learning plan that includes short-term and long-term goals.
- Regularly schedule time for learning activities and stay committed to your plan.

2. Leverage New Skills for Innovation and Career Advancement

Application: Use new skills and knowledge to innovate in your current role or explore new career opportunities. Stay updated with industry trends and technologies to remain competitive and relevant.

Action Steps:
- Research emerging trends in your field and identify skills that are in demand.
- Enroll in courses or workshops that align with these skills.
- Apply your new skills to projects at work or seek new job opportunities that leverage your updated expertise.

3. Pursue Passion Projects and Personal Goals

Application: Identify your passions and interests outside of your current career. Use lifelong learning to turn these passions into tangible projects or new career paths.

Action Steps:

> - Reflect on hobbies or interests you've always wanted to explore.
>
> - Set specific, achievable goals related to these interests (e.g., start a side business, publish a book).
>
> - Take practical steps, such as taking relevant courses or gaining experience, to bring your passion projects to life.

4. Adapt Learning Strategies to Different Life Stages

Application: Tailor your learning approach to your current life stage, whether you're early in your career, mid-career, or approaching retirement. Choose learning opportunities that align with your goals and circumstances.

Action Steps:

> - Assess your current situation and future aspirations.
>
> - Select learning opportunities that fit your stage of life, such as career development courses for professionals or volunteer opportunities for retirees.

- Adjust your learning goals and strategies as your life circumstances change.

5. Utilize a Variety of Learning Resources

Application: Take advantage of diverse learning resources, including online platforms, books, podcasts, and practical experiences. Combining different types of resources can enhance your learning and skill acquisition.

Action Steps:

- Explore various learning platforms and resources relevant to your goals.
- Set aside time for different types of learning activities, such as reading books, watching instructional videos, or engaging in hands-on projects.
- Evaluate the effectiveness of each resource and adjust your approach as needed.

6. Cultivate Resilience and Adaptability

Application: Recognize that setbacks and challenges are part of the learning process. Develop resilience and adaptability to overcome obstacles and stay focused on your learning goals.

Action Steps:

- When facing challenges, analyze the situation and identify potential solutions or adjustments to your plan.

- ➢ Stay motivated by setting realistic milestones and celebrating small successes.
- ➢ Seek support from mentors, peers, or support groups to help you navigate setbacks and maintain progress.

7. Find Learning Opportunities in Everyday Life

Application: Incorporate learning into your daily routines and experiences. Use everyday activities, hobbies, and interactions as opportunities for growth and skill development.

Action Steps:

- ➢ Look for learning opportunities in your daily life, such as exploring new hobbies or engaging in conversations with people from different backgrounds.
- ➢ Reflect on your daily experiences and identify lessons or insights that contribute to your personal growth.
- ➢ Integrate learning into your hobbies, travel experiences, and social interactions to make it a natural part of your life.

8. Set and Monitor Personal Learning Goals

Application: Define clear learning goals and regularly assess your progress. Setting specific, measurable, and achievable goals can help you stay focused and track your development.

Action Steps:

- ➤ Create a list of learning goals related to your personal and professional aspirations.
- ➤ Break down each goal into smaller, manageable tasks with deadlines.
- ➤ Regularly review your progress and adjust your goals or strategies as needed.

Conclusion

By applying these lessons from inspiring stories, you can embark on your own journey of lifelong learning and personal growth. Embrace continuous learning, leverage new skills, pursue passions, adapt to life stages, and use diverse resources to achieve your goals. Cultivate resilience and find learning opportunities in everyday life to make learning a central part of your journey. With dedication and a proactive approach, you can transform your life and achieve significant personal and professional milestones.

Chapter 7
Leveraging Technology for Learning

Digital Tools and Resources

Overview of Useful Apps, Platforms, and Tools for Learning

In today's digital age, technology offers a wealth of resources that make learning more accessible, engaging, and flexible than ever before. From mobile apps to online platforms, leveraging these tools can enhance your learning experience and help you achieve your educational goals. Here's an overview of some of the most useful digital tools and resources available for lifelong learning:

1. Online Learning Platforms

Overview: Online learning platforms provide a wide range of courses and educational content across various subjects and skill levels. They offer structured learning experiences that can be accessed from anywhere at any time.

- **Coursera**: Offers courses from top universities and institutions in various fields, including technology, business, and the arts. Provides certifications and specializations.

- **edX**: Features courses from universities like Harvard and MIT, with options for professional certificates and MicroMasters programs.

- **Udemy**: Hosts a vast library of courses on diverse topics, including programming, design, and personal development, often created by industry professionals.

2. Educational Apps

Overview: Educational apps offer interactive and engaging ways to learn on-the-go. They often include features like quizzes, flashcards, and gamified learning experiences.

- **Duolingo**: A popular app for language learning that uses gamification to teach new languages through interactive exercises.

- **Khan Academy**: Provides free educational content, including video lessons and practice exercises, on subjects like math, science, and humanities.

- **Quizlet**: Allows users to create and study flashcards on various topics, offering different study modes to enhance memorization.

3. Digital Libraries and Book Platforms

Overview: Digital libraries and book platforms offer access to a wide range of books, research papers, and academic journals, enabling in-depth study and exploration of various subjects.

- ➤ **Google Books**: Offers a large collection of books and previews, along with the ability to search within books for specific content.

- ➤ **Project Gutenberg**: Provides free access to over 60,000 eBooks, including classic literature and historical texts.

- ➤ **JSTOR**: Provides access to academic journals, books, and primary sources across various disciplines, often through institutional subscriptions.

4. Online Communities and Forums

Overview: Online communities and forums offer opportunities to connect with others interested in similar topics, share knowledge, and seek advice.

- ➤ **Reddit**: Hosts a variety of subreddits dedicated to different interests and subjects, where users can engage in discussions and find resources.

- ➤ **Quora**: A question-and-answer platform where users can ask questions and receive answers from experts and enthusiasts in various fields.

- ➤ **Stack Exchange**: A network of Q&A websites on topics ranging from programming to cooking, where users can seek and provide expert advice.

5. Interactive Learning Tools

Overview: Interactive learning tools provide hands-on experiences and simulations to reinforce learning and practice skills in a practical context.

- ➢ **Khan Academy Interactive Exercises**: Offers practice problems and interactive exercises to help reinforce concepts learned in video lessons.
- ➢ **Codecademy**: Provides interactive coding exercises and projects to teach programming languages and software development skills.
- ➢ **Tinkercad**: Allows users to create and test 3D designs and electronics simulations, useful for learning design and engineering concepts.

6. Podcast and Video Resources

Overview: Podcasts and video resources offer audio and visual content on a wide range of topics, making it easy to learn while multitasking or during commutes.

- ➢ **TED Talks**: Features talks from experts and thought leaders on a wide range of subjects, providing inspiration and insights on various topics.
- ➢ **YouTube**: Hosts educational channels covering subjects from science and history to DIY projects and coding tutorials.
- ➢ **Podcasts**: Platforms like Apple Podcasts and Spotify offer educational podcasts on diverse topics, providing in-depth discussions and interviews with experts.

7. Virtual and Augmented Reality (VR/AR)

Overview: VR and AR technologies provide immersive learning experiences that can simulate real-world environments or enhance learning with interactive visualizations.

- **Google Expeditions**: Offers virtual reality field trips and educational experiences that allow users to explore historical sites, natural wonders, and more.

- **Anki**: Uses spaced repetition and digital flashcards to help users memorize information more effectively, often used for language learning and test preparation.

Conclusion

Leveraging digital tools and resources can greatly enhance your lifelong learning journey, providing flexible and diverse learning experiences. Whether you're looking for structured courses, interactive apps, digital libraries, or engaging multimedia content, there's a wide range of technology available to support your educational goals. By exploring and utilizing these tools, you can tailor your learning experience to fit your needs and preferences, making continuous education more accessible and effective.

How to Effectively Use Technology to Enhance the Learning Experience

Technology offers incredible opportunities to enhance learning, making it more accessible, engaging, and personalized. To make the most of digital tools and resources, consider the following strategies for effectively incorporating technology into your learning experience:

1. Set Clear Learning Objectives

Strategy: Before diving into various technological resources, define what you want to achieve. Setting clear learning objectives helps you choose the most appropriate tools and stay focused on your goals.

Action Steps:

- ➤ Identify specific skills or knowledge areas you want to develop.
- ➤ Create a list of measurable goals, such as completing a certain number of online courses or mastering a new programming language.
- ➤ Use these objectives to guide your selection of digital tools and resources.

2. Choose the Right Tools for Your Learning Style

Strategy: Different tools cater to different learning styles. Choose platforms and resources that align with your preferred way of learning—whether it's visual, auditory, or kinesthetic.

Action Steps:

- ➤ Assess your learning style: Are you more visual, auditory, or hands-on?
- ➤ Select tools that match your style. For example, if you're a visual learner, consider video tutorials and interactive apps. If you prefer auditory learning, explore podcasts and audiobooks.

- Experiment with different tools to find what works best for you.

3. Create a Structured Learning Plan

Strategy: Develop a structured plan to incorporate technology into your learning routine. A well-organized approach helps you stay on track and make consistent progress.

Action Steps:

- Design a weekly or monthly learning schedule that includes time for using digital tools.
- Set deadlines for completing online courses, reading books, or engaging with interactive exercises.
- Regularly review and adjust your plan based on your progress and feedback.

4. Leverage Interactive and Engaging Tools

Strategy: Interactive tools and resources can make learning more engaging and effective. Use apps and platforms that offer hands-on experiences, simulations, and real-time feedback.

Action Steps:

- Explore tools like interactive exercises on Khan Academy or coding projects on Codecademy.
- Use simulation platforms such as Tinkercad to practice design and engineering skills.
- Engage with apps that offer gamified learning experiences to maintain motivation and interest.

5. Incorporate Multimedia Resources

Strategy: Multimedia resources, including videos, podcasts, and infographics, can provide diverse perspectives and enhance understanding. Integrate these resources to enrich your learning experience.

Action Steps:

- ➢ Combine video tutorials from YouTube with reading materials and interactive exercises.
- ➢ Listen to relevant podcasts during your commute or leisure time to supplement your learning.
- ➢ Use infographics and visual aids to help simplify complex concepts and enhance retention.

6. Utilize Online Communities for Support and Feedback

Strategy: Online communities and forums offer valuable support, feedback, and networking opportunities. Engage with these communities to enhance your learning experience and gain insights from others.

Action Steps:

- ➢ Join forums or groups related to your learning interests on platforms like Reddit or Quora.
- ➢ Participate in discussions, ask questions, and share your progress with community members.
- ➢ Seek feedback and advice from experts and peers to improve your understanding and skills.

7. Track Your Progress and Adapt

Strategy: Regularly track your progress and adapt your learning strategies based on what you've learned. Monitoring your advancement helps you stay motivated and make necessary adjustments.

Action Steps:

- ➤ Use apps or tools that offer progress tracking features, such as course completion statuses and performance analytics.
- ➤ Reflect on your learning achievements and areas for improvement.
- ➤ Adjust your learning plan and resource use based on your progress and changing needs.

8. Balance Technology with Other Learning Methods

Strategy: While technology offers many advantages, it's important to balance digital tools with other learning methods to ensure a well-rounded education.

Action Steps:

- ➤ Complement online courses with hands-on practice, real-world experiences, and face-to-face interactions.
- ➤ Engage in group study sessions or workshops to gain different perspectives and collaborate with others.
- ➤ Apply what you've learned through technology in practical settings, such as projects or volunteering opportunities.

Conclusion

Effectively using technology to enhance your learning experience involves setting clear goals, choosing the right tools, creating a structured plan, and incorporating interactive and multimedia resources. By leveraging online communities, tracking your progress, and balancing digital tools with other learning methods, you can make the most of the technological resources available and achieve your educational objectives. Embrace these strategies to enhance your learning journey and achieve continuous personal and professional growth.

Staying Updated with Technology Trends

Keeping Up with Emerging Technologies and Their Impact on Learning

In the rapidly evolving landscape of technology, staying updated with emerging trends is crucial for maximizing your learning potential. New technologies can reshape how we learn, offering innovative methods and tools to enhance the educational experience. Here's how you can stay informed and understand the impact of these trends on your learning journey:

1. Follow Industry News and Publications

Strategy: Regularly read industry news, blogs, and publications to stay informed about the latest technological advancements and their implications for learning.

Action Steps:

- ➤ Subscribe to technology and education magazines, such as *Wired*, *TechCrunch*, or *EdTech Magazine*.
- ➤ Follow reputable technology news websites and blogs that cover emerging trends and innovations.
- ➤ Sign up for newsletters from educational technology companies and thought leaders.

2. Attend Webinars and Conferences

Strategy: Participate in webinars, virtual conferences, and industry events to gain insights from experts and learn about new technologies firsthand.

Action Steps:

- ➤ Register for webinars and online events focused on educational technology and digital learning tools.
- ➤ Attend conferences and workshops, both virtually and in-person, to network with professionals and explore the latest trends.
- ➤ Take advantage of recorded sessions and resources from these events to access valuable information at your convenience.

3. Join Professional Networks and Online Communities

Strategy: Engage with professional networks and online communities to discuss emerging technologies and share knowledge with peers and experts.

Action Steps:

- ➤ Join LinkedIn groups and online forums related to educational technology and digital learning.
- ➤ Participate in discussions and ask questions about new tools and technologies.
- ➤ Connect with industry professionals and educators to exchange insights and experiences.

4. Experiment with New Technologies

Strategy: Actively explore and test emerging technologies to understand their features and potential applications in learning.

Action Steps:

- ➤ Try out new learning platforms, apps, and tools to assess their effectiveness and usability.
- ➤ Participate in beta testing programs for new educational technologies to gain early access and provide feedback.
- ➤ Experiment with technologies such as virtual reality (VR), augmented reality (AR), and artificial intelligence (AI) to see how they can enhance your learning experience.

5. Leverage Social Media and Online Resources

Strategy: Use social media and online resources to follow thought leaders, tech influencers, and educational technology companies for updates and insights.

Action Steps:

> - Follow relevant hashtags, such as #EdTech or #LearningTech, on platforms like Twitter and LinkedIn.
> - Engage with posts, articles, and discussions about emerging technologies and their impact on learning.
> - Join online communities and forums where professionals share their experiences and recommendations.

6. Participate in Continuing Education and Professional Development

Strategy: Enroll in courses and training programs focused on emerging technologies and their applications in education to enhance your knowledge and skills.

Action Steps:

> - Take online courses or certifications that cover new technologies and their impact on learning, offered by platforms like Coursera or edX.
> - Attend professional development workshops and training sessions focused on integrating new technologies into educational practices.

> Seek out opportunities for hands-on learning and practical experience with emerging tools and technologies.

7. Evaluate the Impact of New Technologies on Learning

Strategy: Assess how emerging technologies are shaping learning environments and their effectiveness in achieving educational outcomes.

Action Steps:

> Review research studies and case studies that analyze the impact of new technologies on learning and education.

> Evaluate the benefits and limitations of technologies based on your personal experiences and feedback from others.

> Stay informed about best practices and guidelines for integrating new technologies into your learning routine.

8. Adapt and Integrate New Technologies Strategically

Strategy: Strategically incorporate new technologies into your learning plan to maximize their benefits and align with your educational goals.

Action Steps:

> Identify specific learning goals and determine which emerging technologies can help achieve them.

➤ Integrate new tools and resources into your learning routine in a way that complements your existing methods and objectives.

➤ Continuously assess the effectiveness of these technologies and make adjustments as needed to optimize your learning experience.

Conclusion

Staying updated with technology trends is essential for leveraging new tools and resources to enhance your learning experience. By following industry news, attending events, experimenting with new technologies, and engaging with online communities, you can stay informed and adapt to emerging trends. Evaluating the impact of new technologies and integrating them strategically into your learning routine will help you make the most of the advancements in educational technology and achieve your learning goals effectively.

Chapter 8
Crafting Your Personal Learning Plan

Developing a Learning Strategy

Steps for Creating a Personalized Learning Plan

Creating a personalized learning plan is essential for effectively achieving your educational goals and ensuring continuous personal and professional growth. A well-crafted plan provides direction, structure, and motivation, helping you stay focused and make consistent progress. Here's a step-by-step guide to developing a learning strategy tailored to your needs and aspirations:

1. Define Your Learning Goals

Strategy: Start by clearly defining what you want to achieve through your learning efforts. Establish specific, measurable, achievable, relevant, and time-bound (SMART) goals to guide your plan.

Action Steps:

> ➢ **Identify Objectives:** Determine what skills or knowledge areas you want to develop. For example, you might aim to learn a new programming language or acquire project management skills.

- ➤ **Set SMART Goals:** Break down your objectives into SMART goals. For instance, "Complete an online course in Python programming within three months" is a SMART goal.

- ➤ **Prioritize Goals:** Rank your goals based on their importance and urgency to focus on what matters most.

2. Assess Your Current Skills and Knowledge

Strategy: Evaluate your existing skills and knowledge to identify gaps and areas for improvement. This assessment helps you understand where to start and how to structure your learning plan.

Action Steps:

- ➤ **Conduct a Self-Assessment:** Reflect on your current competencies and areas where you need development. Use self-assessment tools or feedback from others to gain insights.

- ➤ **Identify Skill Gaps:** Compare your current skills with the requirements of your learning goals to pinpoint gaps.

- ➤ **Create a Skills Inventory:** Maintain a list of your strengths and areas for improvement to track your progress over time.

3. Select Learning Resources and Methods

Strategy: Choose appropriate learning resources and methods that align with your goals, preferences, and learning style. This may include formal education, online courses, books, or experiential learning opportunities.

Action Steps:

- ➢ **Research Resources:** Explore available resources such as online courses, books, workshops, and podcasts related to your goals.

- ➢ **Evaluate Methods:** Consider different learning methods, including formal education, self-directed study, and hands-on practice, to determine what suits you best.

- ➢ **Create a Resource List:** Compile a list of selected resources and methods to incorporate into your learning plan.

4. Create a Learning Schedule

Strategy: Develop a structured schedule to allocate dedicated time for learning activities. A well-organized schedule helps you stay on track and make consistent progress.

Action Steps:

- ➢ **Determine Time Commitment:** Decide how much time you can realistically dedicate to learning each week or month.

- ➢ **Develop a Calendar:** Create a calendar that includes specific learning activities, deadlines, and milestones.

- ➢ **Set Regular Check-Ins:** Schedule regular check-ins to review your progress, adjust your plan, and stay motivated.

5. Establish a Support System

Strategy: Build a support system to help you stay motivated, seek guidance, and receive feedback. A network of mentors, peers, and communities can enhance your learning experience.

Action Steps:

- ➢ **Find a Mentor:** Seek out a mentor or coach who can provide guidance and support in your learning journey.

- ➢ **Join Learning Communities:** Engage with online forums, study groups, or professional networks related to your learning goals.

- ➢ **Share Your Goals:** Communicate your goals with friends, family, or colleagues to create a supportive environment.

6. Track Your Progress and Adapt

Strategy: Regularly monitor your progress and make adjustments to your learning plan as needed. Tracking your achievements and challenges helps you stay on course and improve your strategy.

Action Steps:

- ➢ **Use Tracking Tools:** Utilize tools such as journals, apps, or spreadsheets to record your progress and accomplishments.

- ➢ **Review Milestones:** Regularly review your milestones and goals to assess your progress and identify areas for improvement.

> **Adjust Your Plan:** Be flexible and make necessary adjustments to your plan based on your progress, feedback, and evolving goals.

7. Reflect and Celebrate Achievements

Strategy: Take time to reflect on your learning journey and celebrate your achievements. Reflecting on your experiences helps you recognize your growth and stay motivated.

Action Steps:

> **Conduct Self-Reflections:** Reflect on what you've learned, the challenges you've overcome, and how your skills have improved.

> **Celebrate Milestones:** Celebrate your accomplishments and milestones to maintain motivation and acknowledge your efforts.

> **Seek Feedback:** Gather feedback from mentors, peers, or colleagues to gain additional insights and areas for further improvement.

8. Maintain Flexibility and Continuous Improvement

Strategy: Embrace flexibility and continuously seek opportunities for improvement. Lifelong learning requires adaptability and a willingness to evolve your plan as needed.

Action Steps:

> **Adapt to Changes:** Be open to revising your learning plan based on new interests, goals, or emerging technologies.

> **Pursue Continuous Learning:** Keep exploring new topics and skills to stay engaged and foster ongoing personal and professional growth.

> **Reflect Regularly:** Periodically review and update your learning plan to ensure it remains aligned with your evolving goals and aspirations.

Conclusion

Crafting a personalized learning plan involves defining clear goals, assessing your current skills, selecting appropriate resources, and creating a structured schedule. By establishing a support system, tracking your progress, and maintaining flexibility, you can effectively navigate your learning journey and achieve your objectives. Embrace the process of continuous improvement and reflection to stay motivated and achieve ongoing personal and professional growth.

Setting Short-Term and Long-Term Learning Goals

Setting both short-term and long-term learning goals is crucial for creating a well-rounded and effective personal learning plan. These goals help you maintain focus, measure progress, and stay motivated. Here's how to set and manage these goals effectively:

1. Define Short-Term Goals

Strategy: Short-term goals are specific objectives you aim to achieve within a relatively short period, typically ranging from a few weeks to a few months. They help you make incremental progress and build momentum.

Action Steps:
- **Identify Immediate Objectives:** Determine what you want to achieve in the near future. For example, completing a specific online course or mastering a particular skill within the next three months.

- ➤ **Set Clear Milestones:** Break down your short-term goals into smaller, actionable milestones. For instance, if your goal is to complete a course, milestones could include finishing specific modules or assignments each week.

- ➤ **Create a Timeline:** Develop a timeline for achieving your short-term goals. Use a calendar or planner to schedule your milestones and deadlines.

- ➤ **Track Progress:** Regularly monitor your progress towards your short-term goals. Adjust your plan as needed to stay on track.

Example: If you want to improve your public speaking skills, a short-term goal might be to attend a public speaking workshop and practice delivering a speech in front of a small group within the next two months.

2. Establish Long-Term Goals

Strategy: Long-term goals are broader objectives that you aim to achieve over an extended period, typically six months to several years. They provide direction and purpose for your learning journey.

Action Steps:

> ➤ **Define Your Vision:** Outline what you want to accomplish in the long term. For example, earning a certification in a specialized field or achieving fluency in a new language.

> ➤ **Break Down Goals:** Divide your long-term goals into smaller, manageable steps or phases. This makes them more achievable and helps you maintain focus.

> ➤ **Develop a Roadmap:** Create a roadmap that outlines the key milestones and timelines for reaching your long-term goals. Include major achievements and deadlines along the way.

> ➤ **Regularly Review and Adjust:** Periodically review your long-term goals and progress. Make adjustments as needed to stay aligned with your evolving interests and circumstances.

Example: If your long-term goal is to transition into a leadership role, you might plan to complete a series of management courses, gain experience through leading projects, and build a professional network over the next two years.

3. Align Short-Term and Long-Term Goals

Strategy: Ensure that your short-term goals support and contribute to achieving your long-term objectives. This alignment helps create a cohesive learning plan and maintains motivation.

Action Steps:

- ➤ **Link Goals:** Identify how your short-term goals contribute to your long-term goals. For example, completing a foundational course in a subject (short-term goal) may help you achieve advanced certification (long-term goal).

- ➤ **Set Intermediate Milestones:** Establish intermediate milestones that bridge the gap between short-term and long-term goals. This provides a clear pathway for progression.

- ➤ **Track Progress:** Continuously monitor how your short-term achievements impact your long-term objectives. Adjust your goals and strategies based on your progress and any changes in your plans.

Example: If your long-term goal is to start your own business, short-term goals might include taking entrepreneurship courses, networking with industry professionals, and developing a business plan within the next six months.

4. Create Actionable Steps

Strategy: Develop specific, actionable steps for each goal to ensure clarity and focus. Actionable steps provide a clear path for achieving your objectives.

Action Steps:

- ➢ **Outline Tasks:** List the specific tasks or actions required to achieve each goal. For example, if your goal is to improve your writing skills, actionable steps might include writing daily, reading writing guides, and attending workshops.

- ➢ **Assign Deadlines:** Set deadlines for each task to maintain accountability and stay on track.

- ➢ **Monitor and Adjust:** Regularly review your progress on these tasks and make adjustments as needed to address any challenges or changes in priorities.

Example: For the goal of learning a new software tool, actionable steps might include completing an introductory tutorial, practicing with real-world projects, and seeking feedback from peers.

5. Stay Motivated and Reflect

Strategy: Maintain motivation and reflect on your progress to ensure continued success. Motivation and reflection help you stay engaged and make necessary adjustments to your goals.

Action Steps:

- ➢ **Celebrate Achievements:** Acknowledge and celebrate your accomplishments, both short-term and long-term. This boosts motivation and reinforces your commitment.

> **Reflect Regularly:** Periodically reflect on your progress and experiences. Assess what's working well and identify areas for improvement.

> **Adjust Goals:** Make adjustments to your goals and strategies based on your reflections and evolving interests.

Example: If you achieve a short-term goal, take time to reflect on what contributed to your success and how it supports your long-term goals. Celebrate your progress and use insights to refine your learning plan.

Conclusion

Setting short-term and long-term learning goals provides structure and direction for your personal learning plan. By defining clear objectives, breaking them down into actionable steps, and aligning them with your overall vision, you can effectively progress towards your goals. Stay motivated by celebrating achievements and reflecting on your journey, and make adjustments as needed to ensure continued growth and success.

Tracking Progress

Tools and Techniques for Monitoring Learning Progress and Adjusting Goals

Tracking progress is essential for staying on course with your learning plan and achieving your goals. Effective monitoring helps you assess your achievements, identify areas for improvement, and make necessary adjustments to ensure continued growth. Here's how to track your progress and adjust your goals effectively:

1. Utilize Tracking Tools

Strategy: Employ tools and technologies to systematically monitor your learning progress. These tools can help you record achievements, manage deadlines, and evaluate performance.

Action Steps:

- **Learning Management Systems (LMS):** Use LMS platforms (e.g., Coursera, Udemy) to track course completion, grades, and progress.

- **Project Management Tools:** Employ tools like Trello, Asana, or Notion to manage tasks, set deadlines, and track milestones.

- **Spreadsheets and Journals:** Maintain spreadsheets or journals to record your goals, progress, and reflections. Google Sheets or Microsoft Excel can be particularly useful for tracking data and visualizing progress.

- **Progress Tracking Apps:** Utilize apps specifically designed for tracking progress, such as Habitica, Todoist, or Progress Tracker, to monitor your learning activities and achievements.

Example: If you're working on improving your writing skills, use a spreadsheet to track the number of articles written, feedback received, and milestones achieved, such as completing a writing course.

2. Set Milestones and Deadlines

Strategy: Establish milestones and deadlines to break down your goals into manageable parts. Milestones help you stay focused and motivated by providing regular checkpoints.

Action Steps:

- ➤ **Define Milestones:** Identify key milestones for each goal, such as completing specific modules of a course or achieving a certain level of proficiency.

- ➤ **Create a Timeline:** Develop a timeline with deadlines for each milestone. This helps you maintain a structured approach and stay on track.

- ➤ **Review Progress Regularly:** Schedule regular reviews to assess your progress towards milestones and adjust your timeline as needed.

Example: For a goal of learning a new language, set milestones such as completing introductory lessons, passing intermediate tests, and holding a conversation with a native speaker.

3. Monitor Performance and Feedback

Strategy: Continuously monitor your performance and seek feedback to gauge your progress and identify areas for improvement.

Action Steps:

- ➤ **Self-Assessment:** Regularly assess your own performance against your goals. Reflect on what you've learned and how well you're meeting your objectives.

- **Seek External Feedback:** Obtain feedback from mentors, peers, or instructors to gain insights into your progress and areas for improvement.

- **Adjust Based on Feedback:** Use feedback to make adjustments to your learning plan and address any challenges or gaps.

Example: If you're learning a new software tool, track your performance through self-assessment quizzes and seek feedback from colleagues or instructors on your proficiency and areas for growth.

4. Evaluate and Reflect

Strategy: Periodically evaluate your overall progress and reflect on your experiences. Reflection helps you understand what's working well and what needs improvement.

Action Steps:

- **Conduct Regular Reviews:** Set aside time for regular reviews to evaluate your progress, celebrate achievements, and identify areas for improvement.

- **Reflect on Experiences:** Reflect on your learning experiences, challenges faced, and successes achieved. Consider how these insights can inform your future learning efforts.

> **Update Goals:** Adjust your goals and strategies based on your reflections and any changes in your interests or circumstances.

Example: After completing a major project, reflect on what went well, what could be improved, and how the experience has contributed to your learning goals. Use this reflection to update your goals and plan for future learning.

5. Adjust Goals and Strategies

Strategy: Be flexible and make adjustments to your goals and strategies based on your progress and evolving needs. Adjustments ensure that your learning plan remains relevant and effective.

Action Steps:

> **Review Goals Regularly:** Regularly review your goals and progress to determine if any adjustments are needed. Consider changes in your interests, career goals, or learning preferences.

> **Modify Strategies:** Adapt your learning strategies and resources based on your progress and feedback. For example, if you find a particular learning method isn't working, try a different approach.

> **Update Learning Plan:** Revise your learning plan to reflect any changes in your goals, milestones, or strategies. Ensure that your plan remains aligned with your overall objectives.

Example: If you find that a particular course isn't meeting your needs, adjust your learning plan by exploring alternative resources or modifying your approach to achieve your goals.

6. Celebrate Achievements

Strategy: Acknowledge and celebrate your achievements to maintain motivation and reinforce your commitment to learning.

Action Steps:

- ➢ **Recognize Milestones:** Celebrate the completion of milestones and goals to boost motivation and recognize your hard work.

- ➢ **Share Achievements:** Share your achievements with others, such as mentors, friends, or colleagues, to receive positive reinforcement and encouragement.

- ➢ **Reward Yourself:** Consider rewarding yourself with something meaningful when you achieve significant milestones, such as a new book, a relaxing activity, or a small treat.

Example: After completing a challenging course or achieving a major milestone, treat yourself to a special activity or share your accomplishment with your network to celebrate your success.

Conclusion

Tracking progress involves utilizing tools, setting milestones, monitoring performance, evaluating experiences, and making necessary adjustments. By effectively tracking your progress, reflecting on your achievements, and celebrating successes, you can stay on course with your learning plan and achieve your goals. Embrace flexibility and continuous improvement to ensure ongoing growth and success in your personal and professional learning journey.

Building a Support System

Finding Mentors, Peers, and Communities to Support Your Learning Journey

Building a strong support system is crucial for achieving your learning goals. Having mentors, peers, and communities can provide guidance, encouragement, and valuable feedback throughout your learning journey. Here's how to build and leverage a support system effectively:

1. Finding Mentors

Strategy: Mentors offer valuable insights, advice, and encouragement based on their experience and expertise. They can help you navigate challenges and stay focused on your goals.

Action Steps:
- ➢ **Identify Potential Mentors:** Look for individuals who have experience or expertise in the areas you want to learn about. This could include professionals in your field, educators, or industry leaders.

- **Reach Out:** Approach potential mentors through networking events, professional organizations, or social media platforms like LinkedIn. Be clear about your goals and why you're seeking their guidance.

- **Build Relationships:** Develop a meaningful relationship with your mentor by being respectful of their time, showing gratitude, and actively engaging in discussions. Share your progress and seek feedback regularly.

Example: If you're pursuing a career in data science, seek out experienced data scientists who can offer guidance on career development, skill acquisition, and industry trends.

2. Connecting with Peers

Strategy: Peers provide support, motivation, and shared experiences. They can help you stay motivated and offer diverse perspectives on learning challenges and achievements.

Action Steps:

- **Join Learning Groups:** Participate in study groups, online forums, or local meetups related to your area of interest. Engage with others who share similar learning goals.

- **Collaborate on Projects:** Work with peers on collaborative projects or assignments. This can enhance your learning experience and provide opportunities for feedback and support.

> **Exchange Knowledge:** Share your insights and knowledge with peers and seek their input on your learning journey. This reciprocal exchange can foster a supportive learning environment.

Example: Join a data science study group or an online forum where you can discuss concepts, share resources, and collaborate on projects with other learners.

3. Engaging with Communities

Strategy: Communities offer a broader network of support and resources. Engaging with communities can provide motivation, access to resources, and opportunities for networking and collaboration.

Action Steps:

> **Participate in Online Communities:** Join online communities or forums related to your interests, such as Reddit, Facebook Groups, or specialized platforms like Stack Overflow. Engage in discussions and seek advice from community members.

> **Attend Events and Workshops:** Participate in industry events, conferences, or workshops to connect with like-minded individuals and expand your network.

> **Volunteer or Contribute:** Get involved in community initiatives or contribute to open-source projects. This can provide practical experience and connect you with others in your field.

Example: If you're interested in entrepreneurship, join online entrepreneurial communities, attend startup events, and volunteer for local business incubators to connect with fellow entrepreneurs and mentors.

4. Building a Network

Strategy: Develop a network of contacts who can support your learning journey through various interactions and collaborations. A strong network can provide resources, opportunities, and encouragement.

Action Steps:

- ➢ **Attend Networking Events:** Participate in networking events, industry conferences, or professional meetups to expand your network and make new connections.

- ➢ **Leverage social media:** Use social media platforms like LinkedIn, Twitter, or industry-specific networks to connect with professionals, join groups, and engage in discussions.

- ➢ **Maintain Relationships:** Nurture and maintain relationships with your network by staying in touch, offering support, and sharing updates on your progress.

Example: Attend data science conferences or workshops to meet professionals in the field, connect with them on LinkedIn, and maintain regular contact to stay informed about opportunities and developments.

5. Seeking Accountability Partners

Strategy: Accountability partners help you stay committed to your goals by providing motivation and holding you accountable for your progress.

Action Steps:

> **Find an Accountability Partner:** Choose someone with similar learning goals or interests to act as your accountability partner. This could be a colleague, friend, or fellow learner.

> **Set Up Regular Check-ins:** Schedule regular check-ins with your accountability partner to discuss your progress, challenges, and goals. Provide support and feedback to each other.

> **Share Progress:** Share your achievements, setbacks, and goals with your accountability partner. This transparency helps maintain accountability and motivation.

Example: If you're working on a certification, find a colleague or friend pursuing a similar goal and set up regular meetings to discuss progress, share resources, and motivate each other.

6. Leveraging Resources and Support

Strategy: Utilize available resources and support systems to enhance your learning journey and address any challenges you encounter.

Action Steps:

> **Access Resources:** Take advantage of resources offered by mentors, peers, and communities,

such as recommended readings, course materials, or industry insights.

> **Seek Feedback:** Regularly seek feedback from your support system to improve your skills and understanding. Use this feedback to make adjustments to your learning plan.

> **Participate in Discussions:** Engage in discussions within your support system to gain different perspectives and insights. This can enrich your learning experience and provide valuable support.

Example: If you're learning a new programming language, ask your mentor for recommended resources, participate in coding forums, and seek feedback from peers on your code.

Conclusion

Building a support system involves finding mentors, connecting with peers, engaging with communities, and leveraging resources. By developing a network of support, maintaining accountability, and utilizing available resources, you can enhance your learning journey and achieve your goals more effectively. Embrace the support of others to stay motivated, overcome challenges, and continuously grow in your personal and professional development.

Conclusion

Embracing Lifelong Learning

Summary of Key Takeaways

As we conclude this exploration of lifelong learning, it's essential to reflect on the key strategies and insights that have been discussed throughout the book. Embracing lifelong learning is not just about acquiring new skills or knowledge—it's about fostering a mindset that values continuous growth and development. Here's a recap of the essential points and strategies to help you integrate lifelong learning into your life:

1. Understanding Lifelong Learning

- **Definition and Importance:** Lifelong learning is the ongoing, voluntary, and self-motivated pursuit of knowledge for personal or professional development. It's crucial for adapting to change, enhancing skills, and achieving personal fulfillment.

- **Different Forms:** Lifelong learning encompasses formal education, informal learning, and self-directed learning. Each form offers unique benefits and can be integrated into various aspects of life.

2. The Growth Mindset

- **Concept and Benefits:** Adopting a growth mindset involves believing that abilities and intelligence can be developed through dedication and hard work. This mindset fosters resilience, curiosity, and a proactive approach to learning.

- **Enhancing Learning:** A growth mindset enhances learning by encouraging persistence, embracing challenges, and viewing failures as opportunities for growth.

3. Strategies for Career Advancement

- **For Professionals:** Identifying and acquiring new skills relevant to career growth, and utilizing professional development resources like courses and certifications, can help you stay competitive and advance in your field.

- **For Freshers:** Assessing career-related learning opportunities and building a strong foundation through early experiences are crucial for starting a successful career.

4. Exploring Learning Methods

- **Formal Education:** Traditional degrees and certifications provide structured learning and recognized qualifications that can enhance career prospects.

- **Online Learning and Courses:** Platforms like Coursera, Udemy, and edX offer flexibility and access to a wide range of courses, but it's essential to select high-quality programs that align with your goals.

- ➢ **Self-Directed Learning:** Techniques for self-study, such as using books, podcasts, and online resources, empower you to take charge of your learning journey.
- ➢ **Experiential Learning:** Practical experiences and real-world applications can deepen understanding and enhance skill development.

5. Integrating Learning into Daily Life

- ➢ **Creating a Learning Routine:** Incorporate learning into your busy schedule by setting aside dedicated time and integrating it into daily activities.
- ➢ **Setting Realistic Goals:** Establish achievable learning goals and milestones to track progress and stay motivated.
- ➢ **Finding Learning Opportunities:** Use everyday experiences, hobbies, travel, and social interactions as opportunities for learning.

6. Overcoming Learning Challenges

- ➢ **Common Obstacles:** Address barriers like lack of time and motivation by implementing strategies to stay focused and committed.
- ➢ **Staying Motivated:** Techniques such as setting clear goals, celebrating achievements, and finding accountability partners can help maintain enthusiasm for learning.

- **Dealing with Setbacks:** Learn how to overcome setbacks by reassessing goals, seeking support, and adapting strategies as needed.

7. Inspiring Stories of Transformation

- **Success Stories:** Explore profiles of individuals who have achieved significant personal growth through lifelong learning, showcasing diverse examples from various professions and backgrounds.

- **Lessons Learned:** Key takeaways from these stories highlight common themes and strategies for applying lessons to your own life.

8. Leveraging Technology for Learning

- **Digital Tools and Resources:** Utilize apps, platforms, and tools to enhance your learning experience and stay organized.

- **Effective Use of Technology:** Leverage technology to facilitate learning, stay updated with trends, and access valuable resources.

- **Staying Updated with Trends:** Keep abreast of emerging technologies and their impact on learning to ensure you remain adaptable and informed.

9. Crafting Your Personal Learning Plan

- **Developing a Learning Strategy:** Create a personalized learning plan by setting short-term and long-term goals, tracking progress, and building a support system.

> **Tracking Progress:** Use tools and techniques to monitor your achievements, reflect on your progress, and adjust goals as needed.

> **Building a Support System:** Find mentors, peers, and communities to provide guidance, motivation, and feedback throughout your learning journey.

Conclusion

Embracing lifelong learning is a powerful way to achieve personal and professional growth. By understanding the principles of lifelong learning, adopting a growth mindset, exploring various learning methods, and integrating learning into your daily life, you can continuously enhance your skills and knowledge. Overcoming challenges, leveraging technology, and building a supportive network will further empower you on your learning journey. Remember, the pursuit of knowledge is a lifelong adventure, and every step you take contributes to a more fulfilling and successful life. Embrace the journey, stay curious, and continue to grow and evolve throughout your life.

Encouragement for Ongoing Learning

As we reach the end of our exploration into lifelong learning, it's important to remember that this journey is not just a phase but a continuous part of life. Lifelong learning is a mindset, an ongoing commitment to personal and professional growth that will enrich your life in countless ways. Here are some final thoughts to encourage you to make lifelong learning a seamless and rewarding part of your daily existence:

1. Embrace Curiosity

- **Stay Curious:** Cultivate a sense of curiosity about the world around you. Whether it's delving into a new topic, exploring different perspectives, or trying out a new skill, let curiosity drive your learning journey.

- **Ask Questions:** Never stop asking questions and seeking answers. This inquisitive approach keeps your mind active and open to new knowledge and experiences.

2. Make Learning a Habit

- **Integrate Learning:** Incorporate learning into your daily routine. Allocate specific times for reading, taking courses, or engaging in activities that contribute to your growth.

- **Set Learning Goals:** Regularly set and review learning goals. This helps you stay focused and motivated, and provides a clear direction for your learning efforts.

3. Leverage Opportunities

- **Seek Out Resources:** Utilize various resources available to you, including books, online courses, podcasts, and educational events. Stay proactive in seeking out opportunities for growth.

- > **Learn from Others:** Engage with mentors, peers, and communities to gain insights and feedback. Collaborative learning can enhance your understanding and provide valuable support.

4. Adapt and Evolve

- > **Stay Flexible:** Be open to adapting your learning goals and methods as your interests and needs evolve. Lifelong learning is about flexibility and responsiveness to change.

- > **Embrace Challenges:** View challenges as opportunities for growth. Overcoming obstacles can deepen your learning and strengthen your resilience.

5. Celebrate Achievements

- > **Acknowledge Progress:** Celebrate your achievements and milestones, no matter how small. Recognizing your progress keeps you motivated and reinforces the value of your efforts.

- > **Reflect on Success:** Regularly reflect on what you've learned and how it has impacted your life. This reflection helps you appreciate the journey and encourages continued learning.

6. Inspire Others

- > **Share Knowledge:** Share your learning experiences with others. Whether through mentoring, teaching, or simply discussing what you've learned, inspiring others can enhance your own understanding and reinforce your commitment to learning.

> **Lead by Example:** Demonstrate the benefits of lifelong learning through your actions. Your enthusiasm and dedication can motivate those around you to embrace their own learning journeys.

Final Thoughts

Lifelong learning is a dynamic and enriching pursuit that adds depth and fulfillment to your life. By embracing curiosity, making learning a habit, leveraging opportunities, adapting to change, celebrating achievements, and inspiring others, you create a continuous cycle of growth and development. Remember, the pursuit of knowledge is a lifelong adventure—one that brings joy, empowerment, and endless possibilities. Embrace this journey with an open heart and mind, and let lifelong learning become an integral and rewarding part of your life.

Call to Action

As we close this chapter on lifelong learning, I want to leave you with a powerful call to action. The journey of learning is not a destination but a continuous adventure, and it's never too late to start or reinvigorate your quest for knowledge. Here's a motivational message to inspire you to take the next step:

1. Take the First Step
- **Start Today:** Don't wait for the "perfect" moment to begin your learning journey. Every small step counts. Choose one new skill or topic that excites you and dive in today. Remember, progress begins with action.

2. Commit to Growth
- **Embrace the Journey:** Lifelong learning is a commitment to personal and professional growth. Embrace this journey with enthusiasm and an open mind. Every challenge and discovery along the way will contribute to your development and fulfillment.

3. Set Bold Goals
- **Dream Big:** Set ambitious learning goals that push you out of your comfort zone. Whether it's mastering a new skill, exploring a new field, or pursuing a passion project, aim high and stay dedicated to your goals.

4. Stay Persistent
- **Overcome Obstacles:** Learning is a continuous process that may come with setbacks and challenges. Stay persistent and resilient. Each obstacle is an opportunity to learn and grow stronger.

5. Celebrate Achievements
- **Recognize Success:** Celebrate your milestones and achievements, no matter how small.

Acknowledge your progress and take pride in your efforts. Celebrating your success will fuel your motivation and inspire further learning.

6. Inspire Others

- **Share Your Journey:** As you embark on your learning journey, share your experiences and insights with others. Inspire those around you to embrace their own paths to knowledge and growth.

Motivational Message:

"Your journey of lifelong learning is a testament to your courage, curiosity, and commitment to personal growth. Every step you take, no matter how small, brings you closer to a more fulfilled and empowered life. Embrace the adventure with passion and persistence, and let your quest for knowledge light the way to new possibilities. Start today, stay motivated, and remember that the pursuit of learning is a gift that enriches every aspect of your life. Your journey is just beginning—make it extraordinary!"

Embrace the challenge, celebrate the progress, and let your lifelong learning journey be a source of joy, inspiration, and endless growth. The world is full of opportunities—seize them with enthusiasm and make every moment count.

Appendices

Resources and Tools

To support your lifelong learning journey, here's a curated list of valuable resources and tools across various formats. These recommendations will help you access quality information, enhance your skills, and stay motivated.

Books

1. **"Mindset: The New Psychology of Success" by Carol S. Dweck**
   - A foundational book on the concept of a growth mindset and its impact on personal and professional development.

2. **"Atomic Habits: An Easy & Proven Way to Build Good Habits & Break Bad Ones" by James Clear**
   - Offers practical strategies for forming good habits, breaking bad ones, and mastering the tiny behaviors that lead to remarkable results.

3. **"The Lean Startup: How Today's Entrepreneurs Use Continuous Innovation to Create Radically Successful Businesses" by Eric Ries**

➢ A guide on innovative approaches to entrepreneurship and continuous learning in a startup environment.

4. **"Range: Why Generalists Triumph in a Specialized World" by David Epstein**

   ➢ Explores how diverse experiences and generalist skills can lead to success and growth in various fields.

5. **"Deep Work: Rules for Focused Success in a Distracted World" by Cal Newport**

   ➢ Provides strategies for cultivating deep work habits and maximizing productivity.

Courses and Certifications

1. **Coursera (coursera.org)**

   ➢ Offers a wide range of courses and certifications from top universities and companies. Recommended courses include "Learning How to Learn" and "Introduction to Personal Branding."

2. **edX (edx.org)**

   ➢ Provides high-quality courses from leading institutions. Explore "The Science of Happiness" and "MicroMasters in Data Science" for valuable learning experiences.

3. **Udacity (udacity.com)**

   ➢ Known for its Nanodegree programs in fields like Data Science, AI, and Programming.

Consider "Data Scientist Nanodegree" for in-depth learning.

4. **LinkedIn Learning (linkedin.com/learning)**
   - Offers professional development courses and tutorials in various subjects, including leadership, software development, and design.

5. **Khan Academy (khanacademy.org)**
   - Free educational platform offering lessons in subjects ranging from math and science to economics and humanities.

Websites and Platforms

1. **TED Talks (ted.com)**
   - Features inspiring talks by experts across various fields, providing valuable insights and knowledge.

2. **Medium (medium.com)**
   - A platform for articles and stories on a wide range of topics, including personal development and professional growth.

3. **Skillshare (skillshare.com)**
   - Offers classes in creative fields, business, technology, and more. Explore courses like "Creative Writing" and "Social Media Strategy."

4. **Duolingo (duolingo.com)**
   - A popular app for learning new languages with gamified lessons.

5. Quizlet (quizlet.com)

- ➤ Provides flashcards and study tools for a wide range of subjects, helping with memorization and review.

Tools

1. Evernote (evernote.com)

- ➤ A note-taking app that helps you organize and capture ideas, research, and learning materials.

2. Notion (notion.so)

- ➤ A versatile workspace for note-taking, project management, and organizing learning resources.

3. Anki (apps.ankiweb.net)

- ➤ A flashcard app that uses spaced repetition to enhance memory retention and learning efficiency.

4. Google Scholar (scholar.google.com)

- ➤ A search engine for academic research and scholarly articles across various disciplines.

5. Coursera Learning Hub (coursera.org/learn)

- ➤ A comprehensive hub for exploring courses, specializations, and learning paths.

Using these resources and tools, you can continue to expand your knowledge, stay engaged in your learning journey, and achieve your personal and professional growth goals. Remember, the pursuit of lifelong learning is a rewarding adventure—equip yourself with the best tools and resources to make the most of it.

Templates and Worksheets

To facilitate your lifelong learning journey, here are some sample templates and worksheets. These tools will help you create effective learning plans, set and track goals, and monitor your progress. Feel free to adapt these to fit your personal needs and preferences.

1. Sample Learning Plan

Learning Plan Template

Section	Details
Goal	[Specify your learning goal or objective.]
Learning Outcome	[Describe what you want to achieve or gain from this learning experience.]
Resources	[List the books, courses, websites, and other resources you'll use.]
Start Date	[When you plan to start learning.]
End Date	[When you plan to complete this learning goal.]
Milestones	[Define key milestones or checkpoints.]
Action Steps	[Outline the specific actions or tasks to achieve your goal.]
Evaluation	[Describe how you will measure your progress and success.]

Example:

Section	Details
Goal	Learn Python Programming
Learning Outcome	Ability to build basic applications and understand programming concepts.
Resources	"Python Crash Course" book, Codecademy Python course, YouTube tutorials.
Start Date	August 25, 2024
End Date	October 25, 2024
Milestones	Complete Chapter 1 by September 1, Finish Codecademy course by October 1.
Action Steps	Read chapters 1-3 of the book, complete Codecademy exercises, build a small project.
Evaluation	Review progress weekly, complete a final project to test skills.

2. Goal-Setting Worksheet

Goal-Setting Worksheet

Goal	[Define the specific goal you want to achieve.]
Why It Matters	[Explain why this goal is important to you.]
SMART Criteria	[Ensure your goal is Specific, Measurable, Achievable, Relevant, and Time-bound.]
Action Steps	[List the steps you need to take to achieve this goal.]

Resources Needed	[Identify any resources or support you'll need.]
Potential Challenges	[Anticipate any obstacles you might face and how to overcome them.]
Success Metrics	[Determine how you will measure success.]
Completion Date	[Set a deadline for achieving this goal.]

Example:

Goal	**Write and publish a blog post about Python programming.**
Why It Matters	To share knowledge and build a personal portfolio.
SMART Criteria	Specific: Write a blog post. Measurable: Complete by September 30. Achievable: Research and write. Relevant: Enhances skills and portfolio. Time-bound: Deadline.
Action Steps	Research topic, outline post, write draft, edit, publish.
Resources Needed	Writing tools, blog platform, time for research.
Potential Challenges	Time management, writer's block.
Success Metrics	Blog post published, positive feedback.
Completion Date	September 30, 2024

3. Progress Tracker

Progress Tracker Template

Date	Goal/Task	Action Taken	Progress (%)	Notes
[MM/DD/YYYY]	[Describe goal/task]	[Actions taken or completed]	[Percentage]	[Additional notes or observations]
[MM/DD/YYYY]	[Describe goal/task]	[Actions taken or completed]	[Percentage]	[Additional notes or observations]

Example:

Date	Goal/Task	Action Taken	Progress (%)	Notes
08/30/2024	Complete Python Chapter 1	Read chapter, completed exercises	100%	Chapter was straightforward.
09/15/2024	Finish Codecade my course	Completed all modules and projects	80%	Need to review final project.

Using these templates and worksheets, you can effectively plan, set, and track your learning goals. Customize them to fit your unique learning journey, and use them as tools to keep yourself organized and motivated. Embrace the process, and let these resources guide you toward achieving your lifelong learning aspirations.

Glossary of Terms

This glossary provides definitions of key terms and concepts related to lifelong learning. Understanding these terms will help you navigate the content of this book and apply the concepts to your own learning journey.

1. Lifelong Learning
- **Definition:** The ongoing, voluntary, and self-motivated pursuit of knowledge for personal or professional reasons. Lifelong learning is not confined to traditional educational institutions but occurs throughout life and in various contexts.

2. Growth Mindset
- **Definition:** A belief system, popularized by psychologist Carol Dweck, that suggests intelligence and abilities can be developed through effort, learning, and perseverance. Individuals with a growth mindset embrace challenges, learn from criticism, and persist in the face of setbacks.

3. Formal Education
- **Definition:** Structured learning that typically takes place in an educational institution, such as schools,

colleges, or universities, leading to a recognized certification, diploma, or degree.

4. Informal Learning
- ❖ **Definition:** Unstructured, non-institutionalized learning that occurs through daily activities, interactions, and experiences, such as reading, conversations, hobbies, or exploring new topics out of curiosity.

5. Self-Directed Learning
- ❖ **Definition:** A learning process where individuals take initiative, with or without the help of others, to diagnose their learning needs, set goals, identify resources, choose and implement learning strategies, and evaluate learning outcomes.

6. Experiential Learning
- ❖ **Definition:** A learning process through which individuals gain knowledge, skills, and values from direct experiences outside of a traditional academic setting. This includes internships, volunteering, project-based learning, and real-world applications.

7. MOOCs (Massive Open Online Courses)
- ❖ **Definition:** Online courses designed for large-scale participation and open access via the internet.

MOOCs offer a flexible and affordable way to learn new skills or gain knowledge on a wide range of subjects.

8. Professional Development
- ❖ **Definition:** Continuous training and education that individuals undertake to improve their skills, knowledge, and competence in their professional field. This can include workshops, certifications, conferences, and ongoing education.

9. Learning Styles
- ❖ **Definition:** The preferred way an individual processes information, which can vary from visual (learning through seeing), auditory (learning through listening), kinesthetic (learning through doing), or reading/writing preferences.

10. Microlearning
- ❖ **Definition:** A learning approach that involves consuming content in small, easily digestible chunks. Microlearning is often used for quick, focused lessons that target specific skills or knowledge.

11. E-Learning
- ❖ **Definition:** Learning conducted via electronic media, typically on the internet. E-learning

encompasses a range of online courses, digital tutorials, webinars, and other forms of web-based education.

12. Lifelong Learning Ecosystem
- **Definition:** The network of formal and informal education resources, technologies, and communities that support an individual's ongoing learning journey.

13. Critical Thinking
- **Definition:** The ability to analyze, evaluate, and synthesize information objectively. Critical thinking is essential in lifelong learning as it enables individuals to make informed decisions and solve problems effectively.

14. Upskilling
- **Definition:** The process of learning new skills or improving existing ones to remain competitive in the job market or advance in a career. Upskilling often focuses on acquiring skills relevant to current job roles or future career aspirations.

15. Reskilling
- **Definition:** Learning new skills to transition into a different job role or industry. Reskilling is

especially important in rapidly changing job markets where technology and automation may render certain skills obsolete.

16. Peer Learning

- ❖ **Definition:** A learning process in which individuals learn from and with each other, often in a collaborative environment. Peer learning can occur in study groups, workshops, or community learning initiatives.

17. Learning Management System (LMS)

- ❖ **Definition:** A software platform used to administer, document, track, report, and deliver educational courses, training programs, or learning and development programs. LMSs are commonly used in both educational institutions and corporate settings.

18. Digital Literacy

- ❖ **Definition:** The ability to effectively use digital tools and technologies to find, evaluate, create, and communicate information. Digital literacy is a critical skill in the modern world, enabling individuals to participate fully in the digital economy and society.

19. Soft Skills

- **Definition:** Non-technical skills that relate to how you work and interact with others. Soft skills include communication, teamwork, problem-solving, and adaptability, and are essential for career success and personal development.

20. Cognitive Load

- **Definition:** The total amount of mental effort being used in working memory. Managing cognitive load is important in learning to ensure that new information is processed effectively without overwhelming the learner.

This glossary provides foundational knowledge of key concepts in lifelong learning. Familiarize yourself with these terms as you progress through the book to enhance your understanding and application of the strategies discussed.

A Note of Thanks

Dear Reader,

As you turn the last page of this book, I want to take a moment to express my heartfelt gratitude. This is my very first book, a journey that began with a simple idea and grew into something far beyond what I could have imagined. Your time, energy, and curiosity in exploring these pages mean the world to me.

If this book has resonated with you, inspired you, or even just sparked a small thought, I kindly ask for your support. Please share it with others who might benefit from its message. Perhaps, gift it to someone you care about—because sometimes, the greatest gifts are the ones that help us grow.

I would also love to hear from you. Your thoughts, feedback, and suggestions are invaluable to me as I continue to learn and improve as a writer. Please feel free to reach out to me at saurabh.cegian@gmail.com.

Thank you for being a part of this journey with me. Your support not only means everything to me but also fuels the passion to keep creating, learning, and sharing.

With sincere appreciation,

~Saurabh

www.ingramcontent.com/pod-product-compliance
Lightning Source LLC
LaVergne TN
LVHW061543070526
838199LV00077B/6881